LEON MCKENZIE

CHRISTIAN EDUCATION IN THE 70'S

Modern Perspectives and Approaches in the Teaching of Religion

alba house

A DIVISION OF THE SOCIETY OF ST. PAUL
STATEN ISLAND, NEW YORK 10314

Nihil Obstat:

Daniel V. Flynn, J.C.D.
Censor Librorum

Imprimatur:

James P. Mahoney
Vicar General, Archdiocese of New York
September 20, 1971

The nihil obstat and imprimatur are official declarations that a book or pamphlet is free of doctrinal or moral error. No implication is contained therein that those who have granted the nihil obstat and imprimatur agree with the contents, opinions or statements expressed.

Library of Congress Catalog Card Number: 70-169140

ISBN: 0-8189-0216-7

Designed, printed and bound in the U.S.A. by the Pauline Fathers and Brothers of the Society of St. Paul, 2187 Victory Blvd., Staten Island, N.Y. 10314 as part of their communications apostolate.

CONTENTS

INTRODUCTION

In this age of rapid developments and transitions anyone who puts his ideas down on paper runs the risk of having his words come back to haunt him in a few years. Approaches for Christian education can become dated very easily when scores of religion teachers and writers set themselves to the task of improving the theory, strategies and tactics of Christian education. But the risk is worth the taking. I have tried to be forward-looking to minimize the risks of becoming dated.

This is also the age of complexity. The day is past when one person will be able to devise the perfect program because he has an all-embracing outlook. No individual will be able to claim that he has said the last word about Christian education. Our age of complexity gives birth to an era of pluriformity. We must learn how to take the visions of many men and combine these visions in a personal synthesis. The ideas expressed in the following chapters, then, represent only one point of view. The reader can discover other points of view by referring to some of the books listed in the selected bibliography.

I have attempted to write a book which outlines some basic theoretical principles and suggests some practical advice for religion teachers, pastors and parents. While the book is introductory in nature, I am not so modest as to assume that experts will find nothing worthwhile in these pages. While I have written from the perspective of Roman Catholic Christianity, I would hope that Protestant Christians may find some of my ideas helpful to them.

I wish to thank John F. Wagner, Publisher, for permission to reproduce, in a modified form, an article which appeared in *The Catholic Educator*. I extend my gratitude to Father Victor Viberti, S.S.P., for permission to incorporate some of my material which was previously published in *Pastoral Life*. Both of these men have been most cooperative.

The general content of four of the chapters has been presented previously in print, but I have taken care to update the ideas to correspond with my present views. The remaining ten chapters have not been published before.

Finally, I wish to thank Monsignor Leon A. McNeill for "pestering" me to write this book, and for editing the manuscript. Monsignor McNeill has been enthusiastically involved in Christian education for most of his life; he was well in advance of his time forty years ago — a veritable pioneer in the renewal of Christian education in this country. He encouraged me to begin writing ten years ago; he has been counselor, confidant and coworker — a friend in sunshine and in rain. Whatever good appears in this book can be attributed to his guidance; he is not to be held responsible for any shortcomings in the text. It is with great enjoyment that I dedicate this book to him.

Leon McKenzie
6 November 1971
Caney, Kansas

THE PROCESS
OF CHRISTIAN EDUCATION

The notion of Christian education is complex. We can look at Christian education from various perspectives or points of view, and our definition or description of it will vary with our angle of vision. Shall we define Christian education in terms of teaching or of learning? Shall we view Christian education from the standpoint of methods to be employed or from the standpoint of data to be assimilated by students? Shall we look at Christian education in the light of its aims or in the light of its intellectual content? I suggest that the idea of Christian education is so wide and all-embracing that we must analyze its meaning from many points of view. But before we come to any determination as to the meaning of *Christian* education, we must examine the general meaning of education.

Education: General Meaning

Education is a process. That is to say, education is concerned with a development or movement of the student from one condition to another, from one stage of growth to another. This development is characterized by gradual changes which lead to a desired outcome. The word "process" implies the quality of ongoingness and the factor of the dynamic. The process of education is concerned with the process of human growth. For this reason the process of education suitable for one stage of the student's growth may not at all be suitable for other stages of his growth. The process of education is always relative to the stage of growth at which we find the learner. The word "education" is, therefore, open to many different descriptions.

There are two predominant types of educational process: the spontaneous or unprogrammed process and the structured or programmed process. An example of an unprogrammed process would be the various chemical combinations which take place in the earth's environment to produce, say, oxygen; to produce oxygen through a programmed processing of chemicals in the laboratory would represent professional involvement on the part of man in the chemical reactions which take place. We may simplify the distinction by saying that unprogrammed processes occur more or less "naturally," while programmed processes are more or less artificial, artful or scientific.

In relation to the learning of a language we might say that when a mother relates naturally to her baby by singing and speaking to the child, the process of teaching language has begun in an unprogrammed way. When the child reaches the age for formal education in school, we can say the process of teaching language has become programmed.

Both unprogrammed and programmed processes of education are necessary for the optimal development of the learner. A certain complementarity exists between unprogrammed and programmed educational processes. Unless a child is exposed to some kind of educational process in the home — in the broad sense of the word "education" — he will not ordinarily succeed in a formally programmed educational process. If a child does not experience reality in a peer-group or in a community of learners his own age under the guidance of a teacher, his educational development will not be complete. The existence of Parent-Teacher Associations and Home-School groups testifies to the awareness on the part of educators and parents that both unprogrammed and programmed processes of education must enjoy some form of interplay.

Elements in the Process

There are many important elements in the process of education. Presently we shall examine three of the more important elements: the teacher, the learner and reality. By reality I mean the world outside of the teacher-learner relationship. There also exist relationships between the teacher and reality, and between the learner and reality. The following diagram will show the three elements under consideration and the three major relationships in the educational process.

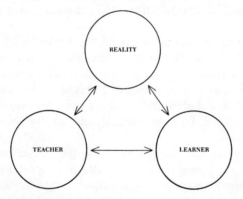

It is the function of the teacher, according to my philosophy of education, to mediate reality to the student; it is the function of the student to bring his life into a positive and rewarding relationship with reality. In order to accomplish the mediation of reality to the student, a relationship of trust and friendship must exist between teacher and student. Since the relationship between teacher and student is for the purpose of communication, and since real communication cannot take place where there is no trust, the quality of the trustful relationship between teacher and student is very important.

The learner, at least in the early stages of the educational process, is not equipped to handle his experiences of reality skillfully or discriminately; he is overwhelmed by the many-aspected face of the outside world; he is unfamiliar with the approaches to reality assumed by the culture in which he lives; he is unable to come to know, understand and interpret the reality outside of himself in an expeditious manner. Certainly the learner *can* learn without the formal help of a teacher; he can profitably enter into communications with others on an informal basis and in an unprogrammed educational process. But such a procedure is most arduous and would tax the energies of the learner to such an extent that he would lose the motivation for learning. This is especially true in the early stages of formal education.

The teacher mediates reality to the student and assists him to interpret his experience of reality; the teacher analyzes, instructs in learning skills, motivates and serves as a model to be imitated. The learner attempts to bring his life intellectually, emotionally and behaviorally into a relationship with reality that is beneficial both to himself and to the community in which he lives.

In the early and middle years of the educational process, ideally in an ever-diminishing pattern proportionate to the growth of the learner, the teacher teaches by direction. In these early stages of the educational process education must be seen chiefly in terms of teaching; after the learner has achieved learning skills and a sense of discrimination, the educational process should be seen principally in terms of learning. When the student attains some degree of maturity and self-motivation, the teacher teaches by indirection.

At the primary grades' level, if the children were permitted to do what they wished, they might well spend the first three or four years of their formal education playing with clay or making faces at each other. The teacher must outline a program of learning skills and basic information which must be assimilated by the children. The children cannot grow intellectually, emotionally or behaviorally to a more advanced stage of human development until they have attained the more fundamental stages. The teacher is directly and explicitly involved in the educational process to the point of dominating it. The good teacher will take into account the enjoyment, entertainment and play that should be inserted into the educational methodology, but enjoyment, entertainment and play are not in themselves the principal desired results of early formal schooling. Children must learn the alphabet, the numbers, good manners, etc.

When the student reaches some degree of proficiency in basic skills and attitudes congenial to learning, he should be given more freedom in determining the educational directions he will take. At the senior high school level, for instance, the teacher should not directly and explicitly mediate and interpret reality to the students who have shown responsibility for learning. Instead, he should be something of a consultant in his special field. Depending on the concrete situation, the teacher should not outline the course of study in fine detail; he should assist the individual students in devising their own study outlines. This approach helps develop creativity in the students. Such an approach is utilized in only a minimal way at less advanced stages of the educational process.

Teachers in all learning fields mediate and interpret reality to the students and assist the students to clarify their experiences of reality. Usually, however, a teacher is concerned with only a specialized area of reality: the reality of grammar, the reality of science, the reality of history, the reality of mathematics and so forth. Specialization and the compartmentalizing of reality into various segments is necessary. Reality needs to be analyzed and "broken up" into pieces, so to speak, small enough for the students to assimilate.

Even the teaching of religion is a specialized area, although references may be made to include other areas of reality in the process of religious education. The religion teacher deals with religious ideas, concepts, traditions and attitudes. But what really distinguishes the religion teacher from other teachers is that he approaches reality in terms of the ultimate meaning of reality, of the world and of human history. In this the religion teacher is much like the teacher of philosophy, but the religion teacher takes as his basic principles of interpretation the systematized beliefs of a formal religious community.

Religious Education

As a teaching specialization, the teaching of religion is not much different from other teaching disciplines; it is different, however, from other teaching disciplines in that it is concerned with the ultimate significance of total reality in the light of particular beliefs or value systems.

Religious education is specified by the basic assumptions, convictions, values and religious affirmations of a religious group. The parents and teachers, as religious educators, teach in accordance with the belief system with which they are affiliated. Thus we can say that Mohammedans, Orthodox Jews, Christians, etc., have different forms of religious education. The specific type of religious education to which the learners are exposed follows upon the specific belief — principles which serve as interpretative norms of reality.

Christian Education

The process of Christian education is a specific type of religious education. The process of Christian education takes Jesus Christ as its fundamental norm for interpreting the ultimate meaning of reality. Christian education is the teaching-learning about reality from a Christian standpoint and on the basis of Christian beliefs and values, as these beliefs and values are articulated and expressed by those who belong to a particular Christian community, e.g., Lutheran, Baptist, Roman Catholic, etc.

The Christian teacher mediates and helps the students to interpret reality. The question is sometimes asked when we speak about the mediation and interpretation of reality: "Are we not supposed to mediate Jesus; are we not to mediate the message of Christ?" The answer to this question is "Yes, but not principally and directly." The principal task of the Christian teacher is to mediate reality to the students in the light of Christ, and to help them interpret reality and their experiences of reality with Christ as the all-surpassing norm of interpretation. It is quite true that the message of Christ as expressed in scripture and doctrine, for example, comes into play. But this is done to enable the students to reach a Christian interpretation of reality. Merely to mediate the message of Christ without reference to the meaning of the world in which we live — and without reference to the ultimate meaning of the world — is to miss the whole point of Christian education. We teach children; we teach young people; we teach adults. We do not teach religion. We employ the data of Christian revelation to teach *people;* we do not teach Christian revelation.

This explanation of Christian education does not put Christ or the message of Christ in a secondary place. On the contrary, this way of looking at Christian education places the message of Christ at the crucial position in the process. The message of Christ stands at the very center of the educational process as the norm by which reality is mediated and interpreted. There is more to Christian education than the mere transmission of words and propositions to the learners. Christian education tries to assist the learners to create a personal relationship to reality which is precisely Christian.

The process of Christian education, then, involves the interpretative mediation of reality to the learner in the light of Christ. The learner's understanding of reality, his attitudes toward reality (and toward himself) and his behavior are ideally transformed when the learner sees reality and his experiences of reality in the light of Christ.

Education or Indoctrination

A few words must be written about the process of indoctrination. Christian education is not indoctrination. This has been noted many times in recent years, but it bears repeating since so many people evidently confuse education with indoctrination. Indoctrination is the mere transmission of information from the mind of the teacher to the mind of the learner. The teacher who indoctrinates works from the basic assumption that the student is a passive receptacle into which "knowledge" is poured. Indoctrination is always mechanistic and regimentalized. The teacher who indoctrinates expects an automatic feedback from the students of those things which have been transferred from the teacher to the students. Thought and reflection are thoroughly uncongenial to the process of indoctrination. Indoctrination requires neither reflection on the part of the teacher nor thought on the part of the students. Indoctrination is not to be identified with declarative statements given by the teacher; indoctrination always implies imperative statements by the teacher which demand acceptance.

It is necessary to underscore the meaninglessness of indoctrination here because some Christian teachers in the past — and in the present — have been more concerned with indoctrination than education, and more feverishly zealous to impart doctrinal formulas or bible stories than to explore reality with the students in the light of Christian revelation. This is not to belittle Christian teachers of the past; it is merely to point out that Christian education has reached a new plateau and has advanced to the point where the futility of indoctrination is now seen clearly. We stand on the shoulders of those who have gone before us. We owe a debt of gratitude to those who have gone before us. But it would be remiss of us not to realize that perhaps some of the shoulders we stand on are slightly stooped. It is equally as fruitless to idealize the past as it is to despise the past. The best way of respecting the past is to move into the future leaving behind us what is no longer useful. Hopefully Christian teachers have left the pedagogy of imperative statement and the process of indoctrination in the past; hopefully they will move into the future in a new way.

Summary

The process of Christian education is concerned with the process of growth of the students. This means that the process will take on different appearances correlative to the different stages of human growth. The teacher is the agent of interpretative mediation of reality for the student.

While teachers in other areas of specialization focus on different aspects of reality, the religion teacher focuses on total reality in the dimension of its ultimate meaning. The Christian teacher mediates and interprets, and helps the students to interpret, reality in terms of Christ as the all-surpassing norm of interpretation.

2

THE AIMS
OF CHRISTIAN EDUCATION

No one begins an enterprise without first intending, at least in some general way, to accomplish a goal or to reach an outcome of his endeavors. Before anyone becomes a teaching participant in the process of Christian education he should have at least some notion of the aims of the process. Or to phrase the matter in another way, intentionality is prior to execution.

We have already seen that the Christian teacher is an agent of the interpretative mediation of reality. This interpretative mediation or interpreted presentation of the world outside of the learner is rooted fundamentally in the recognition and affirmation of Jesus as the all-surpassing norm of interpretation. Jesus is, for humanity, the Father's decisive and final interpretation of reality.

Now the Christian teacher does not *impose* a Christian interpretation of reality upon his students. He avoids imperative teaching and indoctrination. He *proposes* a Christian vision of reality in his act of interpretative mediation, and he assists the learners in *composing* their respective personal Christian interpretations of reality, all of which hopefully fall within the range of orthodoxy and orthopraxis. The learner, it is hoped and desired, will "invent" his personal Christian vision of reality. By "invent" I mean approximately what Pierre Babin means. The learner eventually should be able to be "inventive" enough to find a

way of making faith ". . . . more personal, relevant and interior." [1]
Each believer must respond to God in his own way, while
at the same time attempting to preserve his membership in a
particular Christian tradition. Each believer should attempt to
develop a personal "style" of expressing what the whole Church
expresses or professes. Each believer should grow in his capacity
for faith-response to God.

Faith-growth as Principal Aim

The programmed process of Christian education is one of
the means by which the Holy Spirit elicits from the student
an ongoing, developing and consistent Christlike response to
reality. This response is called the response of faith. Let me
hasten to add here that I have no intention to convey the idea
that the student is to have faith in "reality." But in responding
to the reality of his experience with a Christlike faith the student
is, ultimately, responding to God. God's invitatory call to faith
is "within" every reality-situation that confronts man. It is by
recognizing this call and responding to it with Christlike faith
that the individual actually responds to God.

Faith is not a response to God pure and simple; faith is a
response to God who discloses himself to man in the realities
of man's everyday experiences. By responding to life-situations,
in a Christlike fashion, man utters the response of faith to God.
God reveals himself in reality-situations which confront man;
by responding to reality-situations in a Christlike manner, man
responds to God faithfully.

The aim of Christian education, in a broad sense, concerns
helping the learners "put on Christ" so that they will be able
to respond to the realities in their lives as Christ would respond.
Christian education promotes the growth of the learner's ability
to respond to life in a Christlike manner. Christ is the model
and exemplar for all men. Confronted by the reality of his

---

1. Pierre Babin, **Options**, New York, 1967, p. 89 (footnote).

situation, Jesus responded with total trust and love: he responded in absolute obedience to his Father, even when he knew the path of obedience would lead to his death on the cross. God the Father addressed Jesus in the reality of a situation. By responding to his situation with total trust, love and obedience, Jesus responded to his Father in heaven. Thus we say that the principal aim of Christian education is to help the students conform themselves to the person of Christ, and to assist them to become existentially what they are at least in name: Christians.

The words "help," "assist" and "aid" are of special importance for understanding the teacher's role in accomplishing the aim of Christian education. The Christlike response of the student to the reality of the world cannot be forced or extorted from him. To be valid and authentic the response of Christlike faith must be free and must proceed from the student's autonomous self. It is true that we can coerce students to be present physically for religion class or for religious activities. But it is impossible and futile to think that somehow we can manipulate, say, a high school student into making a faithful Christic response to the realities in his life. This is not to plead that students be given absolute responsibility for their growth in faith, or to suggest that there is never a place in the process of Christian education for firm guidance and strong direction. But I do suggest that despite firm guidance and strong direction, and despite an excellently structured program of Christian education, we cannot expect the automatic accomplishment of the aim of Christian education. Such an expectation or anticipation betrays the intent of indoctrination.

Nor should the teacher become overly discouraged and depressed when it appears that religion classes are not successful. The success of any process of Christian education is attributable ultimately to the Holy Spirit. Lack of apparent success may be due to the teacher's incompetence, but it may also be due to an unreadiness on the part of the student, a previous negative emotional conditioning in regard to Christian education, or to a direct refusal by the student to accept the divine invitation to growth in faith. There is no such thing as a pre-packaged instant Christlike faith we can give to students. The teacher who labors under such an illusion will experience much grief and frustration. The process of Christian education is an ongoing process, and the Holy Spirit produces "results" through the teacher, even in the best of circumstances, only gradually and almost imperceptibly. At least this is ordinarily true. Instant and abrupt "conversions of heart" to Christlike faith are so rare as to be suspect when they do occur.

Three Areas of Faith-growth

The accomplishment of the general aim of Christian education — assistance to the learners for faith-growth — is an accomplishment that ideally takes place in three major dimensions of the human personality.

Educational psychologists have identified three main areas or domains of educational activity: the cognitive domain, the affective domain and the behavioral domain. In the cognitive domain the process of education refers to noetic values, informational data and skills, verbal formulations and concepts; the affective domain concerns the feelings and emotions of the students and their attitudinal orientations; the behavioral domain involves endeavors which enhance the process of education by supporting and/or expressing the cognitive and affective development of the students. In other words, "learning" concerns knowledge, feelings and behavior.

The cognitive domain is best understood in terms of the infinitive "to know"; the affective domain is understood clearly in terms of the infinitive "to feel"; the behavioral domain is understood in terms of the infinitive "to do." Although each of these domains can be speculatively distinguished from the others, they are not really separated in a person. The three domains are interlocking and overlapping. What a person knows, his intellectual convictions, colors his attitudes and inclines him to certain kinds of behavior; how a person feels is related to his cognitive life and to his behavior; what a person does tends to shape his feelings and influence his potential for knowledge. The following diagram will show the inter-relationship of the three learning domains, considered here as domains of faith-growth.

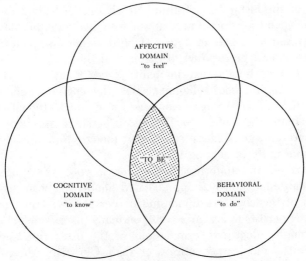

What obtains in each of these three domains converges and is unified in the person — "to be." Thus the following equation can be used to express personality: *To know* + *to feel* + *to do* = *to be.* What a person knows, feels and does, in one sense, defines his personality and identity.

If the faith-growth of the learner is to follow an optimum pattern of development, the process of Christian education must be directed toward the cognitive, affective and behavioral dimensions of his personality. The ongoing and consistent response of faith on the part of the student — the principal aim of Christian education — must be a cognitive response, an affective response and a behavioral response.

In his role as interpretative mediator of reality the Christian teacher should be concerned with informational data which will prove helpful for approaching reality from the perspective of Christian belief. The learner should, *according to his particular stage of cognitive development,* know something of the Bible, he should know something of the normative and privileged doctrinal formulations of the Church, and he should know something of the history of salvation. He should be helped to think critically and abstractly at that stage of his cognitive development when he is able to do so. As he develops and matures the learner should be exposed to theological thinking.

It is unfortunate that in many places today, especially in Catholic high school religion classes, the cognitive domain is neglected in favor of discussion sessions in which students merely ventilate their feelings. Discussion sessions are very good for the exchange of ideas; sometimes, though, they provide only an opportunity of sharing ignorance.

It is equally unfortunate that for so long the process of Christian education was apprehended almost solely in the categories of the cognitive dimension of personality. Much of this thinking persists today. As a result, in many places small children are "taught" doctrinal formulations of the catechism, and this constitutes almost the entirety of their Christian education. I shall have more to say about the process of Christian education for children in a subsequent chapter. Suffice it to repeat here that the process of Christian education must also relate to the affective and behavioral domains of the learner's personality.

Activities in the process of Christian education which are centered around the affective domain are quite necessary. With small children a simple party or songfest or celebration in the environment of the religion class can be most helpful as an experience which aids them to shape their emotional responses to reality in a Christian way. Affective experiences are also necessary for more advanced stages of the process of Christian education. A teacher once structured a learning experience based on an article about a missionary priest and his labors to alleviate human suffering. While the high school students were informed by this learning experience, some of them were also "touched" emotionally in a manner that was quite positive. The books by Doctor Thomas A. Dooley III enjoyed a huge audience among high school students several years ago largely because the reader was "moved" by the doctor's care for the suffering.

I am not saying here that Christian education must become mawkishly sentimental or syrupy; I am insisting that too many religion classes in the past were generally devoid of projects which focused on the faith-growth of the learner in relation to the affective domain of his personality. Perhaps we must convince ourselves that it is something less than human to become so cerebral that we shut off or disparage emotional responses to reality. Our Christlike faith-response to reality should indeed be more than simply emotional, but the emotions have a definite place in the growth of faith.

It was noted above that a person's cognitive capacities and emotions are related to what he does; there is a strong relationship among "knowing," "feeling" and "doing." Because of this there should be planned projects at every level of Christian education which furnish the students with opportunities of "doing." In early childhood various "learning-by-doing" endeavors assist the children in the development of motor or muscular control. At first sight these exercises seem to have little to do with religion. The development of motor control in childhood contributes, however, to the development of interior discipline, e.g., both "mental" and emotional discipline. The famous educator Maria Montessori has written that children are quite interested in bodily movements and that they are eager to discover how they should move about. Children feel that they have mastered their lives to some extent when they have mastered their bodily movements. This period of childhood in which the person learns to coordinate his bodily movements with his mind is a very important period for the development of the total personality.[2]

2. Maria Montessori, **The Discovery of the Child**, Notre Dame, Ind. 1967, p. 90.

Liturgical celebrations constitute another form of "doing" in Christian education. Liturgical activities, in classroom or church, produce an impact in the cognitive and affective domains and serve as ritual rehearsals for everyday Christian life. Much has been written about the liturgy as a pedagogical tool or as an adjunct to the process of Christian education. It would be more appropriate to describe liturgical activity as an integral part of the program of Christian education.

One of the functions of the Church in human history is the diakonic function; that is, the Church must "serve" humanity in order to be true to its very identity as the extension in history of Christ who heals the wounds of human alienation. The "doing" part of the process of Christian education, or the behavioral aspect of the process, should concern "service projects." An example: several years ago a high school CCD group planned a Christmas party for the residents in a home for the elderly. Several class periods were devoted to the collecting of small gifts from local merchants; several other class periods were given over to the practice of the Christmas carols that were to be sung and to the wrapping of the gifts. It seems at the time that much of the activity of the students had little to do with Christian learning. Nonetheless the teacher was able to detect a subtle change taking place in the students. This service project taught them something about reality *vis-a-vis* a Christian interpretation of reality and assisted them in developing a new emotional tone which could be best described as "Christian."

Three Avenues of Mediation

Since there are three domains of learning and, correspondingly, three domains of faith-growth, it follows logically that there

are three avenues of the interpretative mediation of reality that should be followed by the Christian teacher.

As an interpretative mediator of reality in a programmed educational process the Christian teacher must devise projects for each of the three avenues of mediation. It is not always easy to determine precisely that a particular approach is a cognitive approach, an affective approach or a behavioral approach. Ultimately the three avenues converge or blend. But the teacher must at least keep in the back of his mind that there are three avenues of mediation, three leading domains and three areas of faith-growth. He should continually examine his pedagogical conscience to ascertain if his religion class is "weighted" too much in a single domain.

It is necessary also to view the three avenues of mediation in terms of the stages of development of the learners. In early education the affective and behavioral approaches must dominate, and the cognitive approach must be played down. This is simply because the small child is not able or ready to deal with too much cognitive complexity. Likewise, as a child progresses through the grades and on into high school, there should be a steady and progressive emphasis on cognitive approaches. This is not to say that ultimately the affective and behavioral approaches are totally dismissed. A senior high school student may very well be able to deal in profound theological concepts, but his course of study should never become so cerebral that faith-growth in the affective and behavioral domains is neglected.

Perhaps the reader will begin to see at this stage why it is so difficult to define Christian education. Christian education is not one thing; Christian education is many things, relative to the stage of development of the learner. What may pass for good Christian education at the fifth grade level may be very poor Christian education at the tenth grade level.

Summary

The overall aim of Christian education is to assist the students in the growth of faith. This faith-growth ideally occurs in three areas which are correlated to the three domains of learning: the cognitive, the affective and the behavioral. The teacher must analyze his work in terms of the three learning domains and must make every attempt to insure that he directs his interpretative mediation of reality along three paths. He must also emphasize different approaches in the light of the stage of human development at which he finds his students.

3

THE CHRISTIAN TEACHER

The seventeenth century English divine Robert South once stated that the person who governs well leads the blind, but that the person who teaches gives men eyes. As an interpretative mediator of reality, the Christian teacher helps his students become aware of reality and of a Christian vision of reality; he also stimulates and motivates his students to construct a Christian worldview that is at once attuned with Christian orthodoxy and deeply personal. Standing as he does at a crucial juncture of the educative process, the teacher's role is of immeasurable importance. The Christian teacher takes upon himself the challenging task of sharing his faith-insight with others and assisting them to "see" reality from a Christian perspective. He helps his students to develop the "eyes" of faith.

No one questions the fact that good interpersonal relations must obtain between teacher and students; impressionable students are influenced more often by what a teacher is than by what a teacher says. "What you are shouts so loudly," runs the old adage, "that I cannot hear what you are saying." Because of the importance of the teacher in the process of Christian education, we shall dwell on several qualities or characteristics that should be possessed by the teacher. Each of these qualities contributes something to the genesis of an effective Christian teacher; lack of any one of these qualities can spell pedagogical failure. I call these qualities the "Four C's" of the good Christian teacher. The teacher should be: 1) Christian, 2) competent, 3) composed and 4) creative.

The Christian Teacher

When we say that the teacher should be Christian we mean that he must possess, to some degree, what he intends to share with others, namely, a Christian faith. The teacher cannot be merely a nominal Christian; his entire life must consistently be an embodiment of Christ's sermon on the mount. The teacher must have developed an attitude of Christlike response to reality, an attitude that is expressed in his life.

It seems incongruous that a teacher would even attempt to don the mantle of "Christian" educator without having a deep and abiding commitment to Christ, a commitment that touches the core of his personality and influences his very style of living. And yet it is the unfortunate fact that Christian teachers have been recruited in some places without any attention being directed toward their personal holiness. Those who are generous in their contributions to the Church, for example, are not necessarily holier than those who may not be as generous in their financial support.

It is not necessary, nor even desired, that a Christian teacher be a plaster saint or that he overwhelm the students with studied manifestations of piety. But it is a basic requirement that the aspiring Christian teacher is at least making a sincere attempt to live the gospel of Christ and to imitate Christ to the best of his ability. The teacher may experience setbacks and failures in his pilgrimage toward the Christlike ideal, but his whole life is generally oriented toward Christ.

One of the chief ways that the "Christian" commitment of the teacher is expressed in his life refers to his concern for his students. The Christian teacher, without being sentimentally sloppy about it, loves his students and seeks their good. Without compromising his position as their elder or teacher, the Christian teacher accepts his students as friends and affirms the relation of friendship which exists between himself and his students whenever he is able. This does not mean, however, that the teacher becomes a teenager among teenagers or a child among children. Much harm can be done to the teacher-student relationship when the teacher merely becomes one of the students. Most students are quick to see that any teacher who tries to become their "buddy" is engaging in some kind of inauthentic behavior.

So important is the personal Christian faith of the teacher that the absence of this characteristic disqualifies a person as a truly Christian educator. The teacher may fool some of the students by taking upon himself a veneer of Christian life, but eventually most of the students will see through this veneer. Consequently the teacher will be ineffective as a *Christian* interpretative mediator of reality.

The Competent Teacher

Certain levels of competency in the theological sciences should be reached before anyone attempts to become a Christian teacher. The teacher should have some preparation in positive and systematic theology, in scripture and ecclesiastical history.

In his readable book *Understanding the New Theology* Cyprian Cooney explains clearly the distinction between positive and systematic theology. Positive theology is concerned with the "sources" of theology, ". . . usually the written records of the Church." [1] Systematic theology ". . . begins, as it were, where positive theology ends. The believing mind seeks to penetrate the message of revelation for its meaning and relationship to things of human experience." [2] In one sense systematic theology attempts to express and articulate the meaning of reality in the light of Christian revelation. Understandably the teacher must have

1. Cyprian Cooney, **Understanding the New Theology**, Milwaukee, 1969, p. 56.

2. **Ibid.**, p. 57.

some grounding in theology and must be prepared to continue his study of modern theological writers as well as a study of documentation such as pastoral letters and encyclicals.

Scripture represents the privileged and normative literary expression of Christian faith. The teacher must have more than a nodding acquaintance with the Bible. He should know something of the historical contexts in which the books of the Bible were written and something of the various types of literature in the Bible. Nor should the Bible be neglected as a spiritual reading book. One can hardly lay claim to the title of educated person without having read the Bible; a person certainly cannot expect to be an effective Christian teacher without a strong familiarity, at least, with the central biblical themes.

Since the teacher is a mediator of reality *for the learners,* it follows necessarily that the teacher must know something about the learners at their various stages of personal development. Educational psychology, with special emphasis on the religious psychology of children and adolescents, should be studied by the teacher. One of the most serious faults which has been endemic to Christian education for a long time has been the failure to take account of the learner as he really is at different stages of personal development. All too often, for instance, the small child is treated as if he were merely an adult in miniature. Thankfully the relatively new sciences of child and adolescent psychology are the sources of much valuable information for the Christian teacher. Nor should other sciences such as educational anthropology, sociology, and social psychology be overlooked in the preparation of the Christian teacher.

Finally, a certain degree of competency must be achieved in the field of pedagogy, that is, in the area of what to do in a teaching-learning situation: how to use the chalkboard, how to develop lesson plans, how to guide discussions, how to exploit a film for the purposes of Christian education, how to structure a learning experience around a special theme, and a hundred other topics of practical educational value. Pedagogical skills come naturally to a number of people, but most teachers must learn these skills through serious study and under the guidance of a master teacher.

To the beginning teacher it may seem that too much competence in too many different areas is required of him. People usually throw up their arms in despair when they are told how competent they should be. What has been outlined here, of course, refers to *ideal* competency. Teachers should not feel guilty or inferior if they do not meet all of the requirements of ideal competency. They should, however, make every effort to raise the level of their competency.

Several avenues leading to improved competency are open to teachers. Some of the smaller church-related liberal arts colleges offer courses in teacher preparation for Christian education. Unfortunately, the number of these colleges is not too large. The curricular offerings of many of these colleges are woefully inadequate in the category of religious education or catechetical theology. It seems that most church-related colleges have not made a serious attempt to serve the needs of professional religion teachers or volunteer religion teachers in the parishes. The larger church-related universities have excelled in arranging profitable courses for Christian teachers. If it is not too inconvenient, the beginning teacher should seek preparation at one of these universities.

An alternative for teacher preparation that many people find more convenient is participation in summer theological, biblical or catechetical workshops. Much can be gained from these institutes, especially from the association with other religion teachers. Other possible ways of preparing oneself for teaching are attendance at lectures and conferences, participation in co-operative study and discussion programs, taking of home-study courses, private reading and regular meetings with experienced catechists.

More often than not the beginning teacher, and sometimes the experienced teacher, enters into a classroom situation with much trepidation and anxiety. This is particularly true of volunteer religion teachers in the parish setting who teach some form of "Sunday School" or in the CCD program. It is not surprising that teachers who have had little experience in teaching would feel somewhat anxious. But sometimes these feelings of anxiety express themselves in such a way that the students interpret the teacher's attitude as one of hostility.

When a new teacher enters the classroom for the first time he wonders if he will be accepted by the students; he questions whether or not he is competent enough to be a teacher; he is possessed by visions of possible failure. The students themselves experience some form of anxiety when they first meet a teacher. Some students are cautious, hesitant and tense, and sometimes they compensate for these feelings by "acting up." If a teacher shows signs of anxiety, it is possible that these signs will be adjudged as symptomatic of hostility by the students who are ill at ease. In short the atmosphere of hostility will pervade the classroom.

Perhaps it appears that too much is being made here of the need for composure on the part of the teacher and of the necessity of relaxation despite incipient feelings of anxiety. But experienced and knowledgeable teachers will affirm that composure on the part of the teacher is a prerequisite for the establishment of a friendly relationship with students. Arthur T. Jersild, the noted educational theorist, has written that teachers could probably collect much data regarding hostility after they have observed for one week their own attitudes and feelings, and the attitudes and feelings of other teachers.[3]

In Jersild's opinion the teacher can learn to cope with anxiety and to curb both overt and covert hostility by attaining self-understanding. The question of how to use feelings of anxiety constructively and how to arrive at a composed attitude does not fall within the range of our present objectives. The teacher should, however, be aware of the large part played by personal feelings in the process of Christian education and should seek

3. Arthur T. Jersild, **When Teachers Face Themselves**, New York, 1967, p. 117.

insight into causes of anxiousness and fear. Usually the feelings of anxiety disperse after the individual has taught for several weeks. At times it is helpful, especially with adolescents, to admit to them one's feelings of anxiety. Such a procedure at least prevents the students from interpreting anxious movements as signals of hostility.

The Creative Teacher

The creative teacher is innovative and is not afraid to experiment; the creative teacher takes the initiative and on so many occasions relies on personal intuition — on some kind of educational impulsiveness that is productive of clear insight on the part of the students. The creative teacher seizes upon a given situation and turns this situation into a learning experience for the students. The creative teacher can think on his feet and is capable of producing educationally "effective surprises." [4]

How can a teacher become creative? No one knows the complete answer to this question. Perhaps there is a kernel of truth in the opinion that truly great teachers are born and not made. But some guidance can be given concerning the avoidance of those things which impede creativity and produce stagnation.

First of all, creativity is related quite intimately to the personal composure of the teacher, which in turn is related to the self-confidence of the teacher. This self-confidence is bred of feelings of competence and self-understanding. The teacher who is not self-confident is usually very rigid and uncomfortable in the presence of students; he is hardly capable of responding to intuitions for creativity.

Secondly, the teacher must operate in such a manner that he is not tied too closely to prearranged lesson plans. He should

---

4. The creative teacher is one who is capable of producing "effective surprises" which give insight to students. The expression was coined by Jerome S. Bruner. See **On Knowing: Essays for the Left Hand**, New York, 1965.

have a sense of freedom and possess a "freewheeling" teaching style. Several years ago it was the practice of some teacher manuals to schedule the time of the class in such a way that every minute of class time was accounted for. "Five minutes for taking attendance; two minutes for distribution of materials; four minutes for the collection of assignments; eight minutes for review; etc." Even the most secure and proficient teacher, were he to follow such a schedule strictly, would produce little creative fruit. In other words, the teacher must not be fearful of "playing it by ear." Prepare an outline or schedule, by all means, but never fail to depart from the outline when such a departure seems beneficial and promising.

Finally, the teacher who wishes to become creative should not be afraid of making mistakes. Every teacher worth his salt has made mistakes. It is probably true that the person who makes the fewest blunders in the classroom is not saddled with the fear of blundering. When a teacher is acutely conscious of the possibility of failing in an educational experiment, very likely the experiment will never take place. Mistakes will be made; mistakes are made every day by good teachers. But a teacher's mistakes themselves can sometimes become learning experiences for the students. The greatest mistake of the teacher is to fear making mistakes to such an extent that all creativity is thwarted and stifled.

Self-confidence and the composure it effects, assurance of one's competence, the ability to improvise and the quality of being unafraid of experimentation: these are the characteristics of the creative teacher.

Summary

The Christian teacher should be qualified in three basic categories: the spiritual, the academic and the psychological. Spiritually the teacher must be a man or woman of faith, sincerely committed to Christ and to the furtherance of his work in human history. Academically the teacher should be prepared in the sacred sciences and in the educational sciences. Psychologically the teacher must be able to relate to the students and should be free of those inhibitions which curtail pedagogical creativity.

However much any Christian teacher falls short of the ideal, he should be assured that the Holy Spirit of Christ will be with him. This recognition of the place of the Spirit in Christian education should promote hope and should prompt the teacher to spare no effort in attaining the needed qualifications.

4

THE SITUATION
OF CHRISTIAN EDUCATION

One of the most important elements in Christian education is the "situation" in which the process of teaching and learning takes place. The "situation" of Christian education concerns all of those factors which taken together constitute the environment of the educational process. Such factors would be, for example, the time and place of Christian education, the previous experiences of both teacher and students, the sociocultural background of the students, the conditions of the classroom, the availability of sufficient funds for the maintenance of religious education and many others.

It is imperative that all of the factors of the "situation" be recognized and measured before organizational structures of the educational program are established, and before a course outline is developed. The teacher should also plan his teaching strategies with an eye to the educational situation. There are many different ways to approach Christian education, and each of these ways is determined, to a large degree, by the given situation in a particular place.

A few years ago at Fordham University I attended a lecture on modern approaches to Christian education. The lecturer was Father Jacques Audinet, director of religious education at the *Institute Catholique* in Paris. One of the students asked Father Audinet what kind of a program should be developed for a certain diocese in the midwestern United States. The priest replied that he hardly knew the "situation" in New York, much less in the Midwest, and that those who are "on the scene" must analyze the experience of the students in their own life-context before a particular program is developed. One might say, then, that a law of Christian education is that the educational situation is a major determinant of the kind of program which is devised.

There is a growing danger that many teachers will follow published programs and textbook series without any thought to the specific life-context of their students. We can hardly blame publishing houses for failing to produce materials and textbooks that are adequate to all sections of North America. What may speak to the experience of students in New York City may not at all speak to the experience of students in rural Kansas; the approaches that are relevant to the needs of the students in Chicago may not be at all relevant to the needs of the students in New Orleans. The situation of Christian education may change drastically from one parish to another within a diocese or from one place to another in a city. Those who devise programs for specific places must be careful not to accept any predesigned educational program without reference to the concrete situation in which the program will become operative. The key word in this regard is "adaptation." Materials and programs must be adapted to the exigencies of particular situations.

The methods, techniques and strategies to be employed in a classroom for a learning group must also fit the special circumstances of the situation. Perhaps a teacher may find success with a particular strategy in an urban area and failure with the same approach in a rural area. For example, the teacher who habitually plans field trips for students to points of interest in the city may find that such field trips are impossible in rural communities, either because points of interest are too far away or because of the difficulty in arranging transportation for the students. I shall never forget the recommendation suggested by the national office of the Catholic Youth Organization several years ago. Each month the national office mailed suggestions for youth activities to each affiliated parish in the United

States. For one summer month it was advised that a trip to the mountains or to the seashore would be appreciated by the teenagers. This idea struck me as being quite incongruous since our parish was located 700 miles from the nearest mountain and over 1200 miles from the nearest seashore. This example is offered to show that suggested approaches to Christian education must sometimes be rejected in a particular locale.

It would be impossible to cover the entire range of factors which constitute a "situation" within the limits of this chapter. I wish to discuss, in the remaining pages of this chapter, the element of time, the element of place and the usual factors involved in the process of CCD or "Sunday School" type of Christian education.

The Element of Time

The element of time is one of the most important factors that go into the constitution of an educational "situation." In parochial schools care must be taken not to offer religion class at a time of the day when the students are drowsy or when their energies have been spent in other areas of study. To postpone the religion period to the end of the school day is not advised. The students are not alert at this time; their principal interest is the conclusion of the school day and what will happen after the final bell sounds. Also, when religion class is conducted at the end of the day, it seems that the Good News of Christ is merely an addendum to things that are of more value.

The period immediately following lunch is not conducive to real learning. The children are still reviewing in their minds what happened during the post-luncheon recess time and they are unsettled. The section of time immediately preceding the lunch period is also unfavorable to learning; the students are hungry and are more concerned with what they will do during lunch time than with the matter at hand.

The second period of the day — about one hour after school

has begun — is perhaps the most desirable part of the day from the standpoint of readiness to learn. By this time the students have become fully awake; they are ready to concentrate and are physically and psychologically able to pay attention. But even this suggestion is not universally valid. Sometimes an individual teacher may function best at a different time of the day. The determination as to the time of the day for religion class must be made on the basis of many judgments concerning both the teacher's readiness to teach and the learners' readiness to learn.

Should religion class be conducted every day in a parochial school? This question can be answered only by those who are familiar with the specific situation of the school. Perhaps it would be better in some places to conduct religion class only two or three times a week; in other places, particularly when a group of students is blessed with an imaginative and creative teacher, it may be better to conduct religion class every day. If the teacher of young children is incapable of providing learning experiences which touch the affective and behavioral life of the students, and if the religion class is almost totally concerned with the increase of cognitive data, then by all means the religion class should be conducted only once or twice a week. There is simply not that much cognitive data or knowledge that can be assimilated by children in the primary or intermediate grades over the course of an entire year. I shall discuss this at greater length in a subsequent chapter.

There has been an inclination in recent years to advise *all* teachers to conduct religion class only two or three times a week in parochial schools. Sometimes I feel this tendency to diminish the time for Christian education bespeaks uninventiveness or unpreparedness on the part of some teachers. Of course, if the teacher does not know what to do four or five times a week, it is better to reduce the time given to religion class. Nothing is more boring to students than when a teacher constantly "reviews" because of an inability to program new learning experiences for the students.

At the level of the Catholic high school it is almost impossible to state absolutely how often religion class should be scheduled. The problem is even more complicated at the high school level because of a growing number of self-study courses and the introduction of flexible or modular scheduling which departs from the traditional patterns of blocking off time for various subjects. I would suggest, though, that the process of Christian education in the Catholic high school should stress the cognitive domain, i.e., human experience in terms of doctrine, theology, scripture and church history. This means more and not less time is given over to religion class. Once again, the determination as to how much time to devote to Christian education depends on the readiness of teachers and learners and on other elements in the total situation of education.

For the "Sunday School" type of education or the CCD program, the question "how much time?" is fairly well settled. Usually the teacher can be satisfied that students will be allowed one or two hours a week for Christian education, and that this will be what the students will consider "free time." It is necessary, therefore, to devise a program that is interesting enough to overcome the reluctance on the part of the students to attend. The question "what exact time in the week?" must be determined by the parents and teachers. It is a good idea to arrange parent-teacher meetings prior to the opening of the school year for the purpose of determining which time will be most satisfactory to the largest number of people.

Personally, I would stay away from any kind of school situation on Sundays. On Sundays in Protestant churches it sometimes happens that the children and youth are separated from the parents during the time of the worship services. This is not recommended for an extended period of time. Children and youth, although special liturgies can be devised for them occasionally, need the experience of worshipping together in the general community. I shall discuss the place of liturgy in Christian education in fuller detail in a later chapter. In Catholic parishes it is too much to ask children and young people to attend the eucharistic liturgy and then to spend another hour in a classroom situation. Such an approach will be effective only if the educational program is exceptionally interesting for the students.

In some places the time of religious education is Saturday morning for the children in elementary school and Wednesday evening for those in high school. This seems satisfactory to many parents and teachers. Specific circumstances in individual parishes may indicate that some other time would be more feasible.

The Element of Place

Excepting those places to which students go on field trips, the place of Christian education in the parochial school is the classroom. Classes may also be held at times in the parish church when a liturgical celebration is scheduled.

The place for Christian education in a "Sunday School" type program or a CCD program must be determined by those who organize the program. In larger parishes, to which are attached parochial schools, the school can be used on a weekday evening for the high school students and on Saturday morning for the elementary students. Care must be taken, however, that the students do not feel they are interlopers or foreigners. Occasionally it does happen that the students who come to the premises of the parochial school once a week are made to feel as second-class Christians because they are not enrolled at the parochial school on a full-time basis. This occurs in those places where the pastor or parochial school teachers view the parish school as a building constructed primarily for the parochial school students and not as an edifice which is to serve the needs of the entire parish. In one place the principal of the parochial school locked up all audio-visual apparatus and instructional materials. The CCD teachers were forbidden to use the chalkboard and the students were given to know that their presence in the school building was merely tolerated. If such an attitude prevails, it would be better to have no CCD program whatsoever.

In small parishes the various grade levels can be placed in the homes of the teachers, although this approach sometimes works to the disadvantage of the teachers. The high school group can meet in the parish hall or in the rectory, if this is at all possible. When students meet in homes or in the rectory in small parishes, a certain sense of informality and relaxation characterizes the program. This sense of informality can be put to good use by the creative teacher. Much more will be said about the approaches demanded by the CCD situation in a later chapter. It is sufficient to note here that this quality of informality is most necessary for an effective CCD program.

A prime concern when determining the place of Christian education should be the convenience and comfort of the students. It is most difficult for students to become enthusiastic about learning when they are too cold or too warm, when there is too much outside noise, or when they must assume uncomfortable body positions. The place must be well-lighted and acoustically satisfactory. It is most discouraging for students when they cannot see what is happening or when they cannot hear what the teacher or others are saying.

Effective teaching does not always take place in the classroom. Occasionally, weather permitting, it is advised that students be permitted to go outside for class. Much depends, of course, on the availability of space and the presence of attractive surroundings. A teacher would not take a class to a construction site or to a filthy alleyway.

Field trips were mentioned above. Educational excursions are interesting to the students, and much can be learned from such activities. It is advised that the teacher plan the field trip well in advance, notify the parents, schedule adequate transportation, and discuss the impressions of the students at a subsequent class. A field-trip experience is easy for the students to retain in their memories, but their experiences of such an event must be examined and interpreted with the help of a teacher's questions in the class following the field trip. In other words, the field trip is not merely "time-out" from learning but should be integrated into the substance of the teaching-learning plan.

The question of discipline and good order must be considered *vis-a-vis* the field trip. The teacher may be able to deal with a group of twenty or so students in the enclosed area of a classroom, but the same teacher will not be able to give sufficient attention to each member of the group on a field trip. Teacher aides should be recruited to help maintain good order. Good order is especially necessary to maintain on a field trip, not so much for the sake of discipline itself, but for the safety of the students. This is particularly true in regard to children. Regimentation and lockstep precision of arrangement of the group should always be avoided; generally the teacher would be permissive and easygoing. But the welfare of the students sometimes demands firm measures to maintain order.

What kind of field trips can be integrated into the process of Christian education? Just about any kind. One teacher took her students to the Metropolitan Museum of Art in New York City to view the art and artifacts of different cultures. The thrust of the particular lesson was the idea that God is the Father of all men, however different they may be. Another teacher, located in a rural community, accompanied her class to a farm where the children examined the glories of God's creation. One young associate pastor sometimes takes his CCD senior class to various films which are shown commercially in town. The students and the priest discuss the film either at a "Burger Bar" after the movies or in class the following week. The priest exploits certain films to help the students see life in a Christian light.

Summary

The "situation" of Christian education concerns all of those factors which taken together constitute the environment of the educational process. These factors are many in number: the background of teacher and students, the psychological profiles of teacher and students, the specific textbooks that are used and the time and place of Christian education. These latter two factors are quite important. All of the factors which constitute the "situation" of Christian education should be taken into serious consideration before proposing an overall educational program. The "situation" must also be taken into account to enable the teacher to devise effective strategies and meaningful techniques for teaching.

5

PARENTAL INVOLVEMENT IN CHRISTIAN EDUCATION

Over forty years ago, in his encyclical on the Christian education of youth, Pope Pius XI stated emphatically that parents hold directly from God the mission and right to educate their offspring, a right inalienable and anterior to any right of the State or civil society, a right inviolate on the part of any power on earth. The Declaration on Christian Education of Vatican II echoed the ideas of Pope Pius XI. "Since parents have conferred life on their children," the Council proclaimed, "they have a most solemn obligation to educate their offspring. Hence, parents must be acknowledged as the first and foremost educators of their children. Their role as educators is so decisive that scarcely anything can compensate for their failure in it. For it devolves on parents to create a family atmosphere so animated with love and reverence for God and men that a well-rounded personal and social development will be fostered among the children." [1]

The relatively new science of child psychology has arrayed massive evidence supporting the position that the environmental factors of the home play an exceptionally important part in the process of human maturation and education. Religious educators today are firmly convinced that the process of Christian education must *necessarily* include parental involvement and

1. **Declaration on Christian Education**, Section 3.

participation, especially in the years of childhood, if this process is to be ideal, fruitful and effective. This conviction of religious educators is based to a great extent on the data collected by the behavioral scientists.

Child psychologists have shown that the primary center for the assimilation of values and personal life-style is the home. They have shown further that the child begins to assimilate values and imbibe the very atmosphere of the home at a very early age. Some have even speculated that various prenatal influences affect the development of personality and predispose an individual's later religious sensitivities. The Harvard psychologist Erik Erikson takes the position that a person's sense of trust or mistrust begins in the experiences of babyhood which are related to feeding and to the coddling a child receives from its mother. When a child is hungry and cries, it hears the advancing footsteps of mother and then is given its nourishment. In an ill-defined way the baby begins to sense that the world is a reliable place; that it is congenial to human existence. A basic sense of trust begins to develop. Likewise, in cases of children deprived of love and care, a sense of the world's unreliability is engendered, and the child does not build the foundation for trust. Education, in the broad sense of the term, begins in the cradle at some pre-logical and pre-inferential level.

The attitudes and life-style manifested by parents in the home produce an enduring effect on the development of the child's personality. Parental behavior in the home continues to influence the child dramatically as he moves into the years of formal and programmed education and begins to become socialized in peer-groups. Parental attitudes and behavior based on these attitudes constitute a major impact on the evolution of the child's religious life. This is what is meant by the statement that religion is *caught* as much as it is *taught*.

The priest-psychologist Adrian van Kaam points out that it is far easier for us to relate to God and others in a trusting way if we felt ourselves to be loved and accepted by our parents during our childhood. A person who was not loved and accepted by his parents is likely to be fearful that God and other people may reject or condemn him.[2]

Response of Faith

We have seen in a foregoing chapter that the general aim of Christian education is the faith-growth of the students. The Holy Spirit, through the process of Christian education, is able to elicit from the students a living and mature response of faith which results in a strong and consistent relationship of friendship with God. God is always befriending man, and his love is constant; this befriending attitude and constancy of love are not typical of man. He must continually work at developing his faith-relationship with God. And parents must continually assist their children in this work.

The process of Christian education touches man in three dimensions of his personality: the cognitive, the affective and the behavioral. Christian education attempts to assist the development of faith-response by dealing in the intellectual sphere in informational data, in concepts and in the verbal formulations which express the Church's view of reality. The affective or emotional life of man is also a concern of Christian education; Christian education deals with the feelings of students and aims to help them to understand their feelings of love and affection toward God. Activities in the behavioral dimension are gauged to support, express and celebrate Christian understanding of reality and positive religious feelings.

The response of faith and the subsequent orientation of the student's cognitive, affective and behavioral capacities toward God can be anticipated, ordinarily, only when parents collaborate with religion teachers in the work of Christian education. Parents are the primary instruments of God's self-disclosure to children; they are the first signs to the child by which God

2. Adrian van Kaam, **Religion and Personality,** Garden City, N.Y., 1966, p. 12.

communicates his love and elicits and invites the response of faith.

The theologian Bernard Cooke expressed the consensus judgment of Christian educators when he wrote that parental attitudes and the context of the home are of critical importance for the Christian education of children. In the home the child finds his values and his view of the world; the interchanges that take place between the child and his parents, and between the child and his brothers and sisters, can witness the attractiveness of Christianity.[3]

The Christian educator Iris V. Cully has indicated how a positive Christian climate in the home can prepare a child for deep insights into the most profound Christian mysteries. The meaning of redemption, for example, can be known in the relationships which are cultivated in the home. In the home the child is loved for himself; he learns the difference that doing right or doing wrong can make in human relationships; he learns forgiveness and comes to understand, however basically, what God's redemption of mankind means.[4]

Adult Education

Recognizing the importance of the role of parents in Christian education (even before their children are at an age for programmed and formal schooling), most theorists in religious education have expressed the view that adult Christian education is the most urgent need of our times. Some religious educators have even gone so far as to recommend the total concentration of educational efforts in the direction of programs for adults. Others have insisted that since Christianity is an adult religion, the almost exclusive thrust of educational endeavors should be in favor of adults. Such proposals, I believe, are extreme in what they suggest.

3. Bernard Cooke, **Formation of Faith,** Chicago, 1965, p. 62.

4. Iris V. Cully, **Children in the Church,** Philadelphia, 1960, p. 77.

While it may be true that parents must learn of the importance of their role in the Christian education of their children, while they must learn the fundamentals of being good Christian parents, and while Christianity can be defined most adequately from its adult model, it does not necessarily follow that the total or near-total effort of Christian education should be expended for the benefit of adults. What is needed is a vision of Christian education that is all-inclusive and all-embracing rather than selective. The chief priority of Christian education is neither the adult population nor the children; the chief priority for Christian education is simply people.

The real question today is not "How can we cut back on the Christian education of children so we can help adults?" but rather "How can we complete the Christian education of children by completing the Christian education of adults?" Programs that call for the discontinuance of formal Christian education for children must be rejected as something less than pertinent for the needs of the day. As James E. Kraus has written: "All kinds of men, chronologically and intellectually, adults or children, need to hear the word of God. That the full measure of adulthood is the goal goes without question, but hearing the word of God as a child is the instrument which makes him an adult." [5]

What we need is not more Christian education for adults and less for children, but more and better Christian education for everyone. And it is precisely here that catechetical programs for children can contribute to the development of an educational program for adults. We can reach adults by building a program for them into the programs of Christian education for children and adolescents.

Let us admit a basic fact of educational life. Most adults, many of whom are parents, are not interested in adult education programs *per se*. They have little desire to "go back to school."

5. James E. Kraus, **The Living Light**, Vol. 5, No. 2, (Book Review) 1968, p. 129.

These same adults will participate in a program of adult Christian education, however, if such a program has a direct bearing on the practical realities of their everyday lives and on the Christian growth of their children. While the vast majority of parents are not very deeply motivated to attend Christian education programs as such, they are strongly inclined to participate seriously in any program which promises them some practical help in their role of parent-educators.

The filmstrip producer Thomas S. Klise — a remarkable religious educator in his own right — has made the point that religious education programs in church-related high schools can also serve the religious education of parents. If the catechetical program in the high school is at all up to date, teenagers will carry home some of the thought-provoking questions raised by the gospels and the social encyclicals of Pope John and Pope Paul. High school students themselves can serve as catalysts for the ongoing religious education of their parents.[6]

It is all well and good to establish programs of adult Christian education which do not relate to the Christian education of children. A large number of people would possibly be attracted to these programs. But if we are talking about those who have little interest in Christian education as such, then we must attempt to reach these people through their children.

How to Reach Parents

Those who oversee curriculum development for Christian education, either in parochial schools or CCD programs, should search for those textual materials which invite parental involvement. A few catechetical publishing houses have already developed materials which encourage parental participation in the program. To mention two such programs: The Paulist Press "Come to the Father" program for children is a notable example

6. See the letter of Mr. Klise in **Commonweal,** the issue of February 12, 1971, pp. 459 and 479.

of an approach which elicits parental participation through Pastor-Parent-Teacher meetings; the Sadlier "Our Life With God" series includes filmstrips for Parent-Teacher meetings and written guides for parents relating to the "teaching" of religion in the home. In the future we can expect to see all catechetical publishing houses implementing plans in textual materials which call for the inclusion of home religious activities in the process of Christian education. Already those catechetical programs which do not require such parental participation are largely obsolete.

Where it is impossible to adopt textual materials that are designed to allow for parental participation in the total program, the religion teachers themselves should devise a program for parental involvement which addresses itself to the possibilities of a given situation. Parents could be given some help in the area of home instruction of children for first Communion. In one place the parents of children who are preparing for first Communion meet several times in the beginning of the school year to share insights and help solve each other's questions. The parents then instruct their children and permit them to receive the Eucharist when they are ready as individuals.

In another place the religion teachers outlined a series of meetings pertaining to liturgical celebrations in the home. Books, pamphlets and other materials were made available to the parents; they studied the materials, discussed various home liturgies with each other and planned neighborhood liturgies such as the Holy Week paschal meal.

Religion teachers could meet with parents during the course of the school year to discuss the rationale of the particular program of Christian education that is being used. Parent discussion groups could be formed to discuss the central themes the children are learning in the program of Christian education that has been adopted by the parochial school or CCD school. Any number of possible approaches can be employed to assist parents to fulfill their obligations as Christian educators in the home. Indeed, some of the programs devised at a local level,

I suggest, will contain many valuable elements that cannot be found in the programs for parental involvement produced by catechetical publishing houses. Experimental programs created by religion teachers and parents have proven their worth in many places.

Those who teach in the Catholic high school or the parish high school CCD program should also attempt to reach the parents of their students. This is especially necessary today when parents of adolescents are sometimes upset by the new orientations in the teaching of religion since Vatican II. Two types of meetings for parents should be scheduled: 1) programs which concentrate on the new catechetical approaches that are being employed, together with the themes that form the content of the high school course, and 2) programs which deal with areas of concern for parents and their adolescent children. In other words, the first type of program explains to the parents what is being done in religion class and how it is being done; the second type of program relates directly to such concerns as parent-adolescent relationships, the nature of parent-adolescent communication, etc. It is suggested that the first type of program be scheduled early in the school year. Communication between parents and teachers concerning the current approaches in Christian education can solve many problems before they arise.

One group of religion teachers in a CCD situation meets with the parents at the beginning of each semester. At these meetings one of the religion teachers presents a short talk on modern Christian education. The teachers then meet individually with the parents of their students. Toward the end of each semester joint parent-teacher-student meetings are conducted. At these times a special program is presented: a film or filmstrip followed by discussion, a panel of experts, a guest speaker, etc. These programs help establish and strengthen the lines of communication between parents and their children, thereby lessening the gap between generations.

Summary

Parents are the primary educators of their children. As such, they must find a place in the process of formal and programmed Christian education which usually takes place in the school setting. Religion teachers should attempt to include parents in the process of Christian education by selecting textbooks and published programs which take account of parents as primary educators. Should it be impossible for the religion teachers or curriculum committee to adopt textbooks such as these, an attempt must be made to draw up a plan for parent-teacher meetings. Programs for adult Christian education are critically needed today; religion teachers can reach the adult population by structuring meetings which appeal to the natural parental interest in the welfare of children and adolescents.

THE CHRISTIAN EDUCATION
OF CHILDREN

Mary Perkins Ryan, writing in the ecumenical journal *Religious Education*, voiced the opinion that large numbers of Catholics "... have never given up the conviction that religious education at any age really consists in learning the 'truths of faith' encapsulated in tidy doctrinal formulas." [1] She is probably right. One of the most treasured myths of the so-called traditional religious education is the assumption that little children are ready to learn theological formulations and that by memorizing these formulations they are somehow brought closer to God.

It has been said by scores of Christian educators that most programs for children have too much cognitive content; these programs are much too intellectual. With few exceptions those who devise catechetical programs and texts evidently pay little heed to the conclusions of educational psychologists. It seems that many programs and texts for children have been developed with the purpose of treating the children to a *tour de force* in regard to the entire corpus of Christian belief. This is at least true of the "rote memory approach" to Christian education.

Children are presented with abstract theology and complex theological data, couched in seemingly simple language, before they are psychologically able to deal with abstract thinking. In the early grades children are often confused by the simplest

1. Mary Perkins Ryan, "Dr. Goldman and American Catholic Education," **Religious Education**, November-December, 1968, p. 446.

story from the Bible. They pick out insignificant details of biblical narratives and gain a distorted meaning from these narratives. One second grader was asked about his favorite story from the Bible. He liked the story of David and Goliath because the story showed that "little people and children can sometimes get even with big people and parents who punish them." In their book *Creative Teaching in the Church*, Morrison and Foster note that the Bible grew out of adult experience and that we "... cannot assume that a child understands the Bible or appropriates its meaning because he can repeat a few verses from it...."[2] A few years ago the biblical narrative approach was highly recommended; we were told to base our teaching on stories from the Bible. Today we must take a hard look at this approach. Educational psychologists have gathered enough evidence, I think, to support the contention that one must employ Bible stories with much care. When a child attempts to portray the flight into Egypt by drawing Jesus, Mary and Joseph in an airplane, we may be mildly amused. But this total misunderstanding on the part of the child is far from being amusing.

The Concept of Childhood

Many of the theories of the Christian education of the child in the past originated in an inadequate and faulty concept of childhood. Children were supposed to have reached the "age of reason" when they completed their seventh year. It was at age seven that most children exhibited some degree of skill with language. It was thought that this beginning facility with language was a sign of the power of true reflection. "The arbitrary setting of the age of reason at seven years, marking the beginning of the power of rational evaluation of motives and goals, derives from the jurisprudential norms embodied in the ancient

Corpus Juris Civilis of the Byzantine Emperor Justinian I, promulgated in 529 A.D. It is a convenient piece of legalism, but completely untenable in the light of modern developmental psychology." [3]

This fixing of the age of reason at seven years is based on the exigencies of early civil law and not on any secure knowledge or scientifically founded observation. The age seven was selected as a convenience of law and not because anyone really knew at what age a person was capable of rational discrimination. Child psychology tells us something that runs counter to the suppositions of those who framed Justinian's civil law.

Child psychology — as a science employing exact methods — is a relatively recent science. In fact, it is less than one hundred years old. Toward the latter part of the nineteenth century several psychologists began to specialize in the psychology of childhood. Previous to the discoveries of child psychologists many people thought that the child was merely an adult in miniature. It is interesting to note how this assumption is revealed in the fashions of childhood in the last century, and in the depiction of children by artists. In some paintings and woodcuts children are portrayed with the facial features of mature men and women. In 1868 Louisa May Alcott did not find it difficult to write a sentimental romance entitled *Little Women*. Adolescents also were looked upon as somewhat smaller adults.

Modern child psychology has shown us that children are not small-scale adults. Contrary to the assumption in vogue since the time of Justinian, the mental processes of the child are far different from those of the adult. One of the foremost child psychologists, a pioneer in the field, is Dr. Jean Piaget. Piaget spent decades working with children. Basing his descriptions of childhood mental processes on data gathered from testing and scientific observation, Piaget developed a profile of the

3. Robert P. O'Neill and Michael A. Donovan, "Psychological Development and the Concept of Mortal Sin," **Insight**, Fall, 1965, p. 3.

intellectual maturation of the child. He divides the growth patterns of childhood into three principal categories.

1. The Stage of Sense-Motor Operations.
   (birth to two years of age)

At the first stage of development the child learns such things as the coordination of muscular reflexes, the coordination of hand movements with eye movements, the ability to reach for things in order to grasp them. The child learns that some of his activities and movements produce results. The child begins to explore and to experiment. He learns the spatial relationships between various objects.

2. The Stage of Concrete Operations.
   (two years of age to 11 or 12)

During this period the child begins to use his imagination more and more; he acquires language skills and begins, about age seven, simple logic; he begins to reason in a basic and elementary way, but this applies only to concrete objects and not to verbal propositions or abstract statements.

3. The Stage of Formal Operations.
   (begins in early puberty)

This stage is characterized by true problem-solving, reflection, abstract thought, the formulation of general laws for dealing with reality, and the ability to relate abstract propositions one to another without reference to concrete objects. This is what Piaget calls the critical stage in intellectual growth — "critical" in the sense that the person is capable of making authentic rational judgments.

This capsule presentation of the three main stages of intellectual development does not do justice to the enormous work of Piaget. Within these three stages there are many sub-stages. But this broad outline does give us some idea of intellectual development in childhood and may assist us in devising appropriate programs for learning. The implications for Christian education are: 1) There must be a minimization of abstract propositional work until age 11 or 12; 2) Educational programs for children must be activity-centered and must deal with the interpretation of reality in concrete terms.

De-emphasizing "Content"

In the past — in the wake of nineteenth century rationalism and before the data of child psychology was available — children were fed a rather heavy diet of theological propositions. A case in point: the memorization and verbalization of the catechism answers. The emphasis of Christian education was so strong in the cognitive domain that the affective and behavioral domains were almost neglected.

We must realize that the "heart" must be educated as well as the "head." We must underscore the importance of the development of *attitudes* in childhood. "Never mind *how much* the children know in terms of propositions," said one priest. "Never mind how many correct answers they are able to memorize. Most of what the child repeats back to the teacher in religion class is verbalization — the feedback of sounds. Express a few basic truths, familiarize the children with the more important Christian symbols and images, and keep the cognitive element in a secondary place." I must agree with the wisdom of my friend's observation. We will be able to teach "truths" to children and to help them understand reality in the light of these truths in a few years when they are able to understand; when teaching children we must arrange situations for them which will give rise to favorable attitudes.

Now when I suggest a revision of programs for children by de-emphasizing "content" and propositional learning, I am not suggesting that the cognitive elements in education be dropped altogether. But the cognitive elements must be basic and simple. Correlative with the de-emphasis in the cognitive domain there should be an increased emphasis in the affective and behavioral domains. This emphasis can be achieved, I think, by creating educational programs that are activity-centered.

Activity-Centered Education

Bearing in mind that the Christian education of little children involves development of attitudes, and that primary attention must be given to the affective and behavioral domains, we should structure activities through which the children learn. Singing, playing catechetical games, collecting items of religious significance, drawing, making simple Christian symbols out of torn paper or papier-mache, working with clay, finger painting: these activities constitute the essence of Christian education for children. It may well be true that a child who has been exposed to a form of Christian education which places major concern on activities will not be able to pass an examination about abstract religious truths, but this is not the goal of the Christian education of the very young. The goal is the gentle, unrushed nurturing of faith.

In many places, I know, the assumption of the program is that children will increase their knowledge of theological statements which are presented in some kind of language of childrenese. Activity sessions are looked upon not as essential to the learning process but as mere expedients to pass time or to reward the children for being quiet. Religion teachers themselves may feel guilty at times because the children "play" too much in religion class. I submit that programs which stress the attainment of knowledge of abstractions are not only useless but can, at times, become counter-productive to the educational process. The factor of "play" *should* be present in education (at all levels but especially so for children); this is what children excel in doing. When the child is busy doing something that is beyond his comprehension, he becomes easily bored; this leaves a bad taste in his mouth for future adventures in learning. Much of the dissatisfaction of teenagers with religious studies, I propose, stems from experiences in earlier religion classes which were dull and depressing.

It stands to reason that more learning will take place when the program of learning embraces structured situations which are enjoyable and, yes, even entertaining; it is likewise quite reasonable to suppose that little real learning takes place in the early grades when time spent in the religion class is a time of drudgery and ennui. The attention span of small children is stated by educational psychologists in terms of *seconds* and not in terms of hours or even minutes. The attention of children can be focused on learning only if the experience of learning is interesting and appealing.

One key to the creation of appealing learning experiences is movement or activity on the part of the child in the educational process. The children must not sit as passive receptacles into which "knowledge" is poured; they must be actively engaged in the learning experience. Another key is the attention to *objects* in education. According to Piaget the period of concrete operations falls within the 2-11 age range. This is the time when the child is beginning to reason in terms of concrete objects; he is fascinated with the objects he handles, touches and works with.

Perhaps two examples of activity-centered education will help clarify what is meant by this approach. I shall sketch briefly an approach that has proven successful for the primary grades of a CCD program in a large city parish and an approach employed by a fifth grade teacher in a suburban parish CCD school of religion.

Examples of Activity-Centered Education

Before devising a program for primary grade level, the parish priests recruited the teaching personnel and conducted several meetings to explain the activity-centered approach. These meetings were also conducted at various times during the school year. High school girls seemed to have fewer inhibitions about innovation in education, and several young ladies were accepted as teachers. There was an eight-to-one pupil-teacher ratio, which meant that two or three teachers were assigned to the same room.[4]

Classes were conducted each Saturday morning for two hours. The school year ran from the middle of September to the first week in May. Each Saturday morning was divided into eight sections:

1) Singing.

The children began the morning with songs. Fortunately some of the teachers played the piano or guitar. Children's songs and simple hymns were used.

2) Games.

The teachers organized several different games during the year. At times the children were divided into contesting teams. A game that held particular fascination for the children was "catechetical bingo." Each child was given a card with various Christian symbols. As the teacher read a story, mentioning a symbol every once in a while, the children placed markers on the symbols on their cards. (This game may be purchased from Abbey Press, St. Meinrad, Indiana.)

3) Silent Prayer.

Following the "game" section of the class

4. For an informative article on teacher collaboration see "Team Teaching" by Sister Mary Edna, O.L.V.M., in **The Religion Teacher's Journal**, March, 1968, pp. 26ff.

the children were invited to rest their heads on the desk tops and to pray silently to God in their own words.

4) Story.

The teacher would read a story to the children after the period of silent prayer. The stories need not be from the Bible, but an occasional biblical narrative was employed. The story was followed by a short explanatory comment of the teacher.

5) Recess and Refreshment.

Children are very active and cannot remain cooped up in a classroom for too long. They were permitted to take recess on the playground. The teachers played with the children and helped them devise games. Following recess the children were given fruit juice or chocolate milk.

6) Filmstrip.

It is sometimes very difficult to obtain filmstrips which appeal to children. Most of the children were positive in their reaction to the Roa's filmstrip series "Kree Finds the Way" and to Cathedral Films' "Parables of Nature."

7) Laboratory.

In this period of time the children were allowed to select some medium to express something they had learned during the morning. Finger painting, clay, torn paper, drawings, mural work in water colors (on

large papers on the wall), mosaics: all of
these media were available.

8) Singing.

After cleanup, the class ends as it began,
with group singing.

Over the entire year the attendance was figured to be 94.3%.
Some parents observed that their children were enthusiastic
about attending religion class; they also noted that some children
actually cried when they were not allowed to attend because
of sickness or bad weather. This exact program may not be so
successful in all places, but its basic elements should find a place
in all programs.

A Unit on the Exodus Theme

One teacher devised a rather unique way of structuring a
learning experience concerning the exodus of the chosen people
from Egypt. She told the story of the exodus and then wrote
a simple script in which the exodus was re-enacted. Some of
the children prepared places on the playground to represent
various places mentioned in the book of Exodus. Signs bearing
the inscriptions "Sea of Reeds," "Bitter Waters," "Mt. Sinai," etc.
were strategically positioned on the playground. The children
marched, under the leadership of the "Moses" they had elected,
around the playground and back to the schoolroom. A highlight
of this experience was the passover meal celebrated in the schoolroom prior to the "exodus."

It will undoubtedly be objected that such a learning experience is difficult to structure and that it would take too much
valuable time from "classwork." And it will be granted that
such learning experiences can be structured only by teachers who
are willing to spend much time and effort in the exercise of
their creative imaginations. There is no easy way to structure
learning experiences; there is no magic formula. But I must reject

the contention that this type of learning experience takes too much time from "classwork." The children will remember, with delight, their "exodus march." It is doubtful that they would remember abstract statements about the exodus of the chosen people as well as they will remember something in which they were actively involved.

Summary

Because of the clinical discoveries of psychologists about childhood we must replan our programs of Christian education for children. The intellectual "content" of the programs must be de-emphasized in favor of stresses in the affective and behavioral domains. The Christian education of children must be activity-centered. It must involve the children in a direct way. In devising programs teachers should attempt to structure learning experiences which call for the movement of the children and for concrete objects for them to deal with. Of primary importance at this level is the desire to make Christian education an enjoyable experience as well as an informative experience.

7

CHILDREN AND
THE SACRAMENTS

When we speak of preparing children for the sacraments we refer ordinarily to the sacraments of penance, Eucharist and confirmation. In this chapter I shall comment on the sacramental catechesis of children and assert some broad principles on introducing children to the meaning of the sacraments. No attempt will be made to offer a highly defined program, but my general observations will hopefully be of some help to both parents and religion teachers.

Some reference must be made to the theories underlying experimental projects in Christian education today. The reader should take note that the ideas expressed in this chapter represent only the opinions of the author. Furthermore, while I offer suggestions for possible future development in Christian education, I recognize that if there is to be experimentation in liturgical practice, it should be undertaken under the aegis of the local bishop.

No doubt the children in a religion class have already been baptized, but they should know something about the sacrament since all of the remaining sacraments are related directly to baptism. For this reason I begin this chapter with a section on the baptismal catechesis.

But before I consider the sacrament of baptism in terms of the Christian education of children I wish to re-emphasize something that has been stated in a previous chapter. Christian education is not the same as theology, although theology may well come into play at certain levels of the educational process in more or less explicit ways. The purpose of Christian education is not to graduate theologians but to help the students draw near to God. At certain stages of Christian education it is counter-productive to engage in profound theological discussions or to lead the students through metaphysical forests. This is especially true of small children.

Some authors maintain that small children have not reached an age of reflection which permits them to deal efficiently and comprehensively with subtle theological notions. This aptitude for working with complex abstractions, it is maintained, is ordinarily evidenced around age 11 or 12. For this reason it is best to approach the sacramental catechesis of children from the standpoint of religious anthropology rather than from the standpoint of philosophical or theological abstractions. We must concern ourselves not with a rational delineation of the essence of any sacrament but with the child's concrete existence as this existence is touched by sacramental realities. Perhaps the following approach to teaching the meaning of baptism will further clarify what I mean.

An Approach to Baptism

Long before we begin to talk about baptism to children we must be certain that they have at least witnessed the baptismal rite. Experience is the bedrock upon which the edifice of learning is built, and children must have the experience of observing a baptismal ceremony before the teacher begins to discuss the meaning of baptism for their lives. It is advised, therefore, that the teacher arrange for several children to be present when baptism is celebrated in the parish church. This arrangement

1. Cf. section on the growth patterns of childhood, chapter VI, pp. 56-57.

is facilitated in those parishes where baptism is celebrated at Sunday Mass immediately following the liturgy of the word. When the children witness the baptismal ceremony they should be close enough to see what is happening. The symbols of this rite must be permitted to speak to the children.

The initial approach to instructing the children about baptism is the experience of the baptismal rite. The teacher should be prepared to answer questions the children may ask. Baptism should be described, basically, as the special celebration by which the people of god welcome a new Christian into God's family. In baptism we celebrate becoming children of our loving Father; we celebrate the fact that Jesus is our Brother.

Baptism should also be described as God's dramatic call to us to come toward him in loving trust. All of the sacraments are "word-actions" in which God calls us to growth. For the children in the early grades, this explanation is quite sufficient.

As children move into the third or fourth grades — or the analogous level in an ungraded situation — they should examine the symbolism of water. Activities should be structured so that the children will be able to understand the destructive power of water and the life-supporting power of water. God helps us, by virtue of the call he has given in baptism, to destroy what is "bad" in us; he helps what is "good" in us to grow. When fire gets out of hand it is "bad," and water destroys the fire; water is also used to help flowers grow. Baptism is approached in terms of the symbol of water and in terms of the other symbols in the baptismal rite: salt, oil, white garment and candle.

In the middle and upper grades, after the children have attained greater cognitive abilities and have begun to understand the notion of relationship, the cognitive element of the baptismal catechesis may be stressed a little more. Baptism can be presented as a sacred meeting with Christ which helps us to grow toward the Father in love. We come into this world lacking a relationship of love with God. In baptism we celebrate God's love for us and our love for God; we celebrate the beginning of a new relationship of friendship with God.

We cast the baptismal catechesis in terms of personal relationship, friendship and love. The catechesis should remain simple and should avoid difficult theological concepts until the students are able to handle such concepts with more than a marginal competence. We must present baptism as the celebration of God's unconditioned acceptance of us in Christ. In the upper grades we may also present the sacrament against the backdrop of the resurrection. In baptism we die to self and rise again as new men and new women in Christ.

I note again, at the risk of belaboring the point, that theological sophistication regarding the meaning of the sacrament of baptism need not be incorporated too early into the baptismal catechesis. The emphasis of Christian education at the early stages of development in childhood should revolve around concrete symbols and should build upon the child's burgeoning sense of love and his experience of friendship.

Another note of caution. We must be careful in describing the "fall" of man. To interpret the story of man's "fall" in Genesis in its most obvious literal sense can be very confusing to children. When we refer to the story of the "fall" in Genesis we should make it perfectly clear that this is a symbolic story which contains a hidden and significant religious truth.[2] It would be far better, at the level of the upper grades, to show man's "fallenness" and sinfulness by pointing out the presence of evil in the world today. The signals and evidences of the demonic in the modern world should indicate man's need of salvation and his lack of love for God and his fellow men. It was the presence of evil in the world, after all, that prompted

2. This advice does not run counter to orthodox theological formulations regarding original sin. It suggests, however, that the mythopoetic idiom is the best idiom for the education of children. Avery Dulles has reminded us that the abundance of symbolism in the Bible is not accidental and that the "... language of everyday prose would be incapable of mediating the loving approach of the all-holy God with comparable warmth and efficacy" (Dulles, **Myth, Biblical Revelation and Christ,** Washington, D.C., 1968, p. 6).

the author of Genesis to attempt to explain as he did, under divine influence, the origin of sin and evil, and man's awareness of alienation from his brothers and from God.

After examining the ritual of baptism and the symbols employed in this ritual, the teacher should, in essence, show that evil is a reality in our lives, that Christ came to destroy evil, and that we celebrate our victory and Christ's victory over all evil in the solemnization of baptism. Baptism, furthermore, is a special call to each of us to grow in love and to draw closer to God. Nothing more is required, at the elementary level, to assist children to understand the meaning of their lives in the context of Christian baptism.

The Eucharist

Traditionally children were prepared for first confession before first Communion. I wish to pass on to a consideration of the basic preparation needed for first Communion. I will show in a subsequent chapter why I feel first confession should come some time after first Communion.

The elements of the eucharistic catechesis are few in number. The child should be familiar with some of the major aspects of the life of Jesus. He should have some general idea that Jesus is the Son of God and that he is our savior; that Jesus was crucified for our wickedness and died for our sins; that the Father raised Jesus from the dead as a sign to humanity that the Father accepts us; that Jesus commanded us to love God and our neighbor as ourselves.

After the children have been introduced to Jesus, some time should be spent explaining the Mass to them. Again, the explanation must be simple and appropriate to the mental capacities of the children. The Mass we celebrate in our parish church points back to the last supper, to the sufferings and death of Jesus and to his resurrection from the dead. The Mass points forward to the glorious celebration we shall enjoy with Jesus in the future. The Mass is a special celebration of the followers of Jesus. In the Mass the priest repeats the last supper. Jesus is present for us in the bread of the Eucharist. When we partake of the eucharistic bread, Jesus enters our hearts and we talk to him as we would talk to our best friend.

There is no need, when preparing a child for first Communion, to place undue stress upon details about fasting. All too often the child becomes greatly confused if we attempt to fill his head with too many particulars. We must remember we are dealing not with miniature adults but with children.

As the child grows and advances through the grades of elementary schooling, the eucharistic catechesis can be examined in further detail. The historical roots of the last supper — the Seder or passover meal — can be analyzed and perhaps celebrated in the classroom. The meaning of the Eucharist as a sign symbolizing and effecting unity can be discussed. The eucharistic catechesis must be biblical and should refrain from metaphysical or theological explanations of the mode of Christ's presence in the Eucharist. There is a difference, I propose, between teaching theology and preparing small children for first Communion. The catechesis should concentrate on the Old Testament types and foreshadowings of the Eucharist and should reflect New Testament notions. The religion teacher may profitably arrange learning situations which explore and examine the symbolism of bread and wine.

When I suggest that the catechist should refrain from metaphysical or theological explanations of the mode of Christ's presence in the Eucharist I am not implying a rejection of that theological approach which attempts to explain the mode of Christ's real presence. I prescind entirely from the question of the most adequate way of explaining the real presence theologically. Whether we should speak of the real presence in the language of transubstantiation, transignification or transfinalization is not the concern of small children. It suffices to state that Jesus is really present in the Eucharist and that he abides in us when we receive him in Communion.

As children advance in elementary Christian education, the

ecclesiastical law of fasting before receiving Communion can be explained in greater detail to them. This is not to say that the ecclesiastical law of fasting is unimportant; it is to take into account, however, the fact that small children have an inclination to confuse essentials with non-essentials. How many of us, in the "old days" worried about going to Communion because some raindrops fell on our tongues on the way to church? Similarly the question of serious sin *vis-a-vis* reception of the Eucharist can be explained more fully in the context of the catechesis on penance. (We shall treat this in greater detail in the next chapter.)

Children and Confirmation

In some places the sacrament of confirmation is being "postponed" until the students reach adolescence. This practice has been opposed by some who argue that children should receive confirmation soon after their first Communion so as to be strengthened by the confirmational grace of the Holy Spirit. "If the child is confirmed by age nine or ten," the argument goes, "he will be furnished with special graces to assist him in the years of adolescent turmoil. Besides, if we do not confirm the children while they are in elementary school, it may happen that they may never receive the sacrament later on."

It is certainly true that the sacraments confer grace *ex opere operato* and that the efficacy of the sacraments is not substantially affected by the personal dispositions of the minister of the sacraments. If a priest in serious sin, for example, celebrated the Eucharist, the sacrament would still be "valid." Jesus would still be present in the Eucharist. But when we say the sacraments make grace available *ex opere operato* we must not think that this is some fancy theological terminology used to describe a magical process. The sacraments are not magic. Catholic theology has always stipulated that the effect of the sacramental encounter is conditioned by the dispositions of those who received the sacraments.

Now it is doubtful that small children have reached an appropriate age to celebrate their Christian maturity in the sacrament of confirmation; it is likewise doubtful that they can become appropriately aware of the call to a fuller Christian maturity which God addresses to them in the sacrament of confirmation. In other words, the dispositions required for a most fruitful reception of confirmation are not present in children.

It is almost ludicrous at times to hear a bishop addressing a confirmation class of second graders. He calls them to witness the gospel of Christ in a mature way in the marketplaces of the world. Many bishops do not even address their remarks to the children but to the parents instead. The incongruity of confirming children becomes quite evident at the celebration of this sacrament.

Confirmation is a sacrament of Christian maturity — a *rite de passage* similar to the Jewish *bar mitzvah* ceremony which marks the entrance of the adolescent boy into the synagogue as one who has reached a basic level of maturity. And yet in many places the sacrament of confirmation bears little relationship to the reality of the lives of those who are confirmed. The sacrament of confirmation, sad to say, has become in many places something of a theatrical spectacle which is hardly understood by those who are receiving this sacrament.

As a rite of passage into the adult world the sacrament of confirmation should be made available to those who wish to restate their baptismal vows and to commit themselves publicly as mature people to the gospel of Christ. This means that people should not be encouraged to receive confirmation at least until they are of high school age. A few years ago, in the diocese of Rochester, Archbishop Fulton J. Sheen suggested that confirmation be postponed until age 17 or 18. Happily other bishops are following this example and are waiting until people are equipped with adequate dispositions before the sacrament of confirmation is celebrated.

By waiting until high school age before celebrating the sacrament of confirmation, the confirmation catechesis for children is simple and brief. The children are merely told that they will be given an opportunity when they are older to affirm their baptismal vows and to celebrate their growth in Christ. They should know that the Holy Spirit will come to them sacramentally at a later time to afford his special assistance — an assistance which enables them to enter into the adult life of the Church and to continue to grow in this Christian life.

Marriage, Holy Orders, Anointing

When children are in the middle to upper grades of elementary school, they should be given a brief explanation of the sacraments of marriage, holy orders and anointing of the sick. It has never been shown that children are closer to God because they have a facility to rattle off the names of the seven sacraments. I propose that by the time of sixth, seventh or eighth grade — depending on the overall catechetical situation — the children should know something about all of the sacraments. I propose further that undue emphasis should not be placed on the catechesis of marriage, holy orders and the anointing of the sick because these sacraments do not touch upon the immediate experiences of children. It is axiomatic among educators that experience is the foundation for learning and that students excel in learning when interest is present. Children do not manifest interest to any great degree in the sacraments under discussion. A more complete catechesis on these sacraments should be given during the high school years when the students are thinking about marriage, vocation in life and the limitations of being human.

8

CHILDREN AND PENANCE

In the past — at least that part of the past we tend to identify with what is "traditional" — children were prepared for first confession at the same time they were prepared for first Communion. The religion teacher would teach the children the formula for confession, the proper terminology for various sins, a basic theology of the sacrament and how to recite the act of sorrow. Not a small amount of time was spent instructing the children in the rudiments of moral theology, i.e., the difference between mortal and venial sins, the things that make a sin mortal and so forth.

Today the practice of admitting children to the sacrament of penance at an early age is slowly being replaced. Some priests and religious educators, basing their judgment on the insights of modern child psychology and on pastoral experience, suggest that the first formal confession of sin should not take place until age 13 or 14. Others do not wish to postpone first confession until early adolescence, but they do agree that the catechesis of penance should be separated completely from the eucharistic catechesis.[1] All too often in the past the attention

1. It must be noted that the recent Catechetical Directory issued by the Congregation of the Clergy recognizes the possible validity of postponing first confession from an early age. In permitting authorized experimentation the Catechetical Directory does not rule out the theories put forward by some modern educational psychologists.

of the children was concentrated too much on what was to be said and done in the first confession. This resulted in a less than optimum appreciation of the Eucharist. The highlight of the week of first Communion was not the Eucharist but rather the experience of first confession, an experience which was sometimes unsettling and even terrifying.

I mentioned above that the practice of postponing confession for children grew out of the re-examination of the sacrament of penance in the light of modern child psychology. Two landmark monographs published in 1965-66, co-authored by a priest and a psychologist, treat extensively and perceptively "The Question of Preadolescent Sin." [2] In the following paragraphs I shall rely heavily on ideas proposed in these articles.

The authors show that a child is not capable of committing serious sin because: 1) the child lacks the ability of true abstract thought; 2) the child lacks the ability to understand sufficiently the notion of "relationship" with God; 3) the child lacks the ability of true critical and evaluative thinking. These deficiencies of ability in childhood thinking are substantiated by the data of clinical psychologists, and chiefly by the work of Jean Piaget.[3] It is noted that not just any kind of reasoning power is necessary for the guilt of sin to be imputed but ". . . a full and perfect use of reason which suffices for deliberation regarding serious matters, for discerning moral good and evil, for choosing a goal in life, and so forth." [4]

The presumption that a child reaches the age of reason is just that, a presumption. The age of seven was arbitrarily selected as the age of rational discernment by the lawyers who

2. Robert P. O'Neil and Rev. Michael A. Donovan, "The Question of Preadolescent Sin," **Insight: Quarterly Review of Religion and Mental Health**, Spring, 1966, pp. 1-10.

3. Two of Piaget's works are especially valuable: **The Moral Judgment of the Child**, Glencoe, Ill., 1948, and **Judgment and Reasoning in the Child**, New York, 1928.

4. O'Neil and Donovan, **op. cit.**, p. 5.

compiled the ancient law code of Justinian in 529 A.D. The principles and presumptions of this code of civil law influenced the legal thinking of most of the Mediterranean world. Indeed, the canon law of the Church shows the profound influence of the Justinian code. The notion that a child of seven is responsible before the law was simply accepted by Church lawyers when the Church assimilated to itself much of the culture of the Roman empire. This acceptance of an arbitrary legal fiction influenced the pastoral practice of the Church to the extent that small children — at least in relatively modern times — were generally admitted to the sacrament of penance. "The gross anomaly is apparent to any thinking person: while no court in the modern world would even indict (much less condemn to capital punishment or life imprisonment) a child under the age of ten, we teach that an All-just and All-merciful God and Father . . . will send them to hell for all eternity for an act which they conceivably might commit."

The argument for postponing first confession until the child is older seems highly valid. The validity of the argument takes on even greater force when we consider the Christian education of children *vis-a-vis* their image of God. God must be presented as a loving Father. To bring too emphatically into the catechesis of children the concepts of sin and punishment makes it difficult for children to imagine God as a loving Father. An early and immoderate emphasis on sin, punishment and the justice of God will make many children insecure and fearful of anything that is linked with religion. "It would be ill-advised . . . to have the child associate the name of God with fear, punishment and even threats . . . . The child should not be haunted by the idea that God is angry with him. His religion should be one of love: it is not fear that should inspire his desire for good, but love of God. The child needs to know that no matter what happens, he is always loved by God." [5]

5. Xavier LeFebvre and Louis Perin, **Bringing Your Child to God,** New York, 1963, p. 82.

While the authors of the foregoing passage are speaking about the three- and four-year olds, what they state applies unequivocally to the general Christian education of children. A happy, secure childhood, particularly regarding religious affections and emotions, is the foundation of a happy Christian life. The child must learn to trust others and the world in which he lives, and this learning must take place in the first few years of childhood. This ability to trust can later be exercised in reference to God. In order to build the capacity to trust in childhood, the child should be loved, accepted and affirmed; the child should be taught that he is loved, accepted and affirmed by God. Later the matter of sin and punishment for sin can be explained, and then in terms of man's self-punishment and acceptance of the consequences of sin. God should never be presented as the one who takes vindictive pleasure in punishing his children; the punishment due to sin is self-imposed and self-inflicted — a concept that is impossibly difficult for children to understand.[6]

Discipline and Moral Instruction

Although a child may not be capable of incurring the guilt of serious sin, he does occasionally perform acts which are materially wrong. When a child does something wrong he should be told that such behavior is not appropriate. A child needs rules to live by and he needs discipline. But the discipline must always be of such a character that it does not defeat the child's self-esteem and crush him emotionally. Dr. Haim G. Ginott's best-selling book *Between Parent and Child* offers many valuable insights for correcting the misbehavior of children. The book should be read by every parent and religious teacher.

Dr. Ginott suggests that when correcting children the parent (or teacher) must state what behavior is unacceptable and also what behavior is permitted. A substitute behavior, in other words, should be taught. "You may not throw dishes; you may

6. Cf. Richard McCarthy's **Does God Punish?**, New York, 1968.

throw pillows. Or in less grammatical but more effective English: Dishes are not for throwing; pillows are for throwing. Brother is not for boxing; Bobo is for boxing." [7] When correcting a child the statement of correction must not be interpreted by the child as an attack upon his worth.

Suppose a mother enters the bathroom and finds her child splashing water on the floor. If the mother loses her temper and cries out, "What are you doing, you naughty child!" the child may well interpret this statement as an indication that mother has withdrawn her love. Instead, the mother should remain as calm as possible and should say, "Water is not for splashing in the house; water is for splashing in the pool or at the beach." The child will learn that splashing water in the house is unacceptable behavior without fearing that he has been abandoned by his mother.

This approach is effective also with adolescents. Many of the freshmen boys at a certain high school were given to the practice of shooting paper clips with rubber bands. One teacher apprehended a boy *in flagrante delicto* and began to lecture him. "This fad of shooting paper clips must stop. Haven't you any regard for anyone else? What kind of immature oaf are you? Don't you know that you could harm someone? Is that what you want to do, put someone's eye out?" The boy sulked in the corner of the room for the remainder of the period. Before the next period began, at the interval between classes, he was again shooting paper clips. This time another teacher caught him in the act. The teacher maintained his composure and said, "Paper clips are not for shooting people with; paper clips directed at others can harm them." The boy paused, smiled slightly and turned his rubber band and paper clips over to the teacher. The teacher responded, "People who shoot paper clips are punished by staying after school." The boy shook his head acknowledging that he got the message.

The first teacher made a point of discussing the personality

7. Haim G. Ginott, **Between Parent and Child,** New York, 1969, p. 116.

of the student. The student felt as if he were under attack. The second teacher remained calm and instead of discussing the personality of the student he discussed the improper use of paper clips and the punishment for such improper usage. That is, the second teacher approached the situation *objectively;* the first teacher put his correction of the student on a highly *subjective* basis.

The misdeeds of children, then, must be corrected even if the guilt of these misdeeds is not imputed to them. They must be corrected in such a way that they do not lose their self-esteem or feel rejected by the one who does the correcting. The consequences of misdeeds should be explained to children in a language that is appropriate to their age. If a child is mean to his pet, he must be told that pets are not for hitting with a stick; he must be told that pets are to be cared for because they depend on us just as children depend on parents. If a child is caught telling a lie, he should be told that the tongue is for speaking the truth with. How terrible it would be if people everywhere did not tell the truth; children would never trust their parents when parents promised a treat. The consequences of misdeeds, as the reader may have observed, should be explained in the context of the child's home experience.

Frequently there is a tendency among parents and teachers to explain why certain behavior is not permitted by a reference to God. Children should not be told "God will punish you for misbehaving" or "Lying hurts God." Before children learn the consequences of their misdeeds in reference to God, they must learn the consequences of their misdeeds in reference to others. It is by developing a Christian attitude concerning others that we develop a loving relationship to God.

Gradual Preparation for Confession

I am not suggesting here that the penitential catechesis of children be postponed because first confession is postponed.

I am suggesting, however, that children be prepared for first confession gradually. Father William F. Allen has outlined a penitential catechesis for children that deserves our attention. He writes that children in the first grade should be taught that God is all-loving and merciful. God asks all of his children to be good and to do certain things. A person does wrong when he says "no" to God. But God is always ready to forgive anyone who says "no." "A contrast between family situations and the sin-God situation should be drawn and the essence of love shown to be in forgiveness such as the child experiences at home." [8]

During second grade the child should be encouraged to examine his actions and attitudes toward others. Children should be told that they are responsible for their actions and attitudes. The love of God for sinners must also be stressed. "The third grader is to be introduced to these same concepts perhaps a little more deeply." [9]

The fourth grader should be instructed as to what constitutes sin in daily situations of life. "The malice of sin will be underlined. But the horror of sin will not have a deleterious effect upon the child because he knows the great God as a God of love and mercy . . . . He should be encouraged to private confession. In these confessions let the child confess as he would in his own language and surely not insist on number and kind of sin." [10]

Group penance celebrations are helpful in preparing the child for first confession. The celebrations may take place any time from first grade until the time for first confession. Ordinarily such a celebration begins with a song or hymn. This is followed by readings from the Bible. Readings that speak of

8. William F. Allen, "Quid in Casu?", **Pastoral Life**, November, 1967, p. 62.

9. **Ibid.**

10. **Ibid.**

God's goodness and mercy, e.g., the parable of the prodigal son, are particularly valuable. After the readings a short homily is given by a priest or religion teacher. The children are then asked to spend a few moments in silence thinking about the times they said "yes" to God and the times they said "no." They should be instructed to seek God's forgiveness and mercy in the silence of their hearts. After the brief period of meditation the priest or religion teacher should pronounce a simple blessing over the children. The celebration is concluded with another song or hymn. Over a period of a few years the children gradually come to a realization of the meaning of sin and an understanding of sorrow and God's mercy. When they make their first confession they will be ready for a fruitful sacramental encounter with Christ.

A word of caution must be directed to priests and religion teachers. Although children are not disturbed when first confession is postponed, the parents of these children sometimes have severe doubts and reservations. Some parents are not emotionally able to accept changes in "traditional" patterns of sacramental practice. These parents should be permitted to prepare their own children for first confession at age seven or eight, if they so desire. In other words, this change in sacramental practice should not be forced on parents. Parents should be instructed as to the desirability of postponing first confession till at least the end of the 4th grade or even later; they should be helped to understand the reasons for its postponement. But under no circumstances should they be constrained to act against their better judgment. It sometimes happens that the home life of the child is disrupted when priests or religion teachers argue with parents over the most appropriate time for first confession. Parental distress is very easily transferred to children. If a parent is anxious or distressed about the change in sacramental practice, this anxiety or distress will be picked up by the child. The result will be that first confession will be even more productive of anxiety for the child.

History of the Sacrament

Of all the sacraments perhaps none has undergone more changes in liturgical practice than the sacrament of penance.[11] In the early Church, in some local communities, it was necessary to confess only the sins of adultery, murder or apostasy; this confession was made to the bishop, who prescribed a penance. In still other times and places a person was permitted to receive the sacrament of penance only once in his lifetime. The satisfaction imposed on the penitent was generally public in nature. Public confession of sins, while not required, was sometimes permitted.[12]

St. Augustine noted that the giving of alms, good works and prayer were traditional ways of expiating daily sins, and that confession was the ordinary means of forgiveness of serious sins. The local Council of Agde in 506 cautioned that penance was not to be given readily to young people because of the inconstancy of youth.

From the seventh to the tenth century the practice of sacramental penance underwent profound changes. The Irish monks who evangelized continental Europe introduced the practice

11. I rely particularly on Peter Riga's **Sin and Penance**, Milwaukee, 1962, for most of the information on the history of the sacrament of penance.

12. "The origins of auricular confession are obscure; it is old, at least as old as the patristic period, but it was not the original discipline of penance. The literature of the early Church speaks only of the public administration of penance, and it dealt only with serious sins. The offender confessed his sin before the entire congregation and received a severe penance, which might include fasting, exclusion from the Eucharist, the wearing of sackcloth and ashes, and prostration under the feet of the congregation. Tertullian believed that murder, adultery, and idolatry could not be forgiven by ecclesiastical penance. The belief was unorthodox, but it did not imply a denial that these sins were forgiven by God; it simply stated that the Church was not empowered to forgive them . . . ." (John L. McKenzie, **The Roman Catholic Church**, New York, 1969, p. 160).

of private and more frequent confession. The element of spiritual direction in the private confession of sins tended to increase the frequency of the celebration of this sacrament.

I mention the changes in the practice of sacramental penance only to show that the practice of the recent past has not been characteristic from the very beginning of the Church. Pastoral practice regarding the sacrament of penance seems to have depended on the exigencies of a particular time and place.

Summary

In many places today children are not being admitted to the sacrament of penance at an early age. Because of the insights of modern psychology, it is now thought that critical and evaluative thinking does not begin to take place until pre-adolescence or early adolescence. Children need rules to live by and they need correction. Correction of misdeeds should be given in such a way that the child's self-esteem is not threatened. Children should be prepared for first confession only gradually. Parents should not be upset by this change in pastoral practice. In the light of the past history of the sacrament, change seems to be quite common and dependent upon the insights of each succeeding age.

TEACHING TEENAGERS: STRUCTURES

When we speak of Christian education at the secondary or high school level we must distinguish immediately whether we are talking about Christian education in the Catholic high school or Christian education in the parish CCD program. Our approaches to teaching-learning and our structures of organization will not be the same for both of these situations. A daily continuity obtains in the Catholic high school religion class; this continuity is not usual in the parish CCD program. Again, the teachers in a Catholic high school are, in most cases, professionally trained as teachers, while the teachers in the parish CCD program are ordinarily recruited from among members of the parish; they — the CCD teachers — devote some of their leisure time to the work of Christian education.

In this chapter I wish to outline some approaches to the Christian education of teenagers that I have found promising. Obviously it will be impossible to consider the entire range of programs which are noteworthy. Further, I wish to limit my considerations to the matter of structuring the organization of programs for the Catholic high school and for the parish CCD program. Sometimes the very quality of Christian education is improved through the improvement of organizational structure.

The Catholic High School

During the past several years the notion of elective programming in religious studies has won the accolades of many religious educators.[1] Elective programming meets the specific needs of a catechetical situation and takes advantage of specific opportunities. All too often the adoption of a textbook series for high school religious education results in dissatisfaction on the part of both teachers and students. No single textbook series or schema of themes suggested by a textbook series can possibly be adequate to the exigencies of each and every high school.

The reader will recall from a previous chapter that Christian education focuses on the intellectual, emotional and behavioral domains of the human personality. The elective program should be created with the end in view of providing course offerings which encompass all three of these learning domains. It is most difficult to achieve a perfect balance of cognitive, affective and behavioral elements in a single course of studies, although this can be accomplished. Sometimes a course offering will lay special accent on one of the domains to the near exclusion of the others. Balance can be achieved, however, in a religious studies *curriculum* that strives for the harmonious interaction of cognitive, affective and behavioral elements.

How is an elective program devised? Usually the religion teachers at a high school come together to share insights for an elective program. They should keep in mind three factors: 1) the needs and interests of their students; 2) the capabilities and limitations of the teachers; 3) the opportunities and limitations of the concrete situation in which they are working.

It would be a waste of time to construct a course of study that would have no appeal to the students. Eventually the unappealing courses — and the poor teachers — are weeded out when students fail to select the unappealing courses or poor teachers. It would also be foolish to devise a course of study

1. For a more complete review of electives in high school religion classes see **Ideas for Electives in High School Religion** by Sr. Deborah Lorentz, S.S.S., and Rev. Elwin Schwab. The book is published by Geo. A. Pflaum.

which is beyond the competencies of any of the religion teachers. Finally, those who build an elective program must be aware of the physical assets and liabilities of the school and the availability of adequate resources such as books and audiovisual aids.

Perhaps it would be helpful to reproduce a brief outline of courses offered in an elective program by two cooperating Catholic high schools in the Midwest. The two schools share faculty members and exchange students.

Freshman Year

No electives are offered in the first year. The religion course is built around a survey of biblical literature and a study of Church history. The freshman year serves as a foundation for the elective courses which follow in subsequent years.

Sophomore Year

The electives are minimal. This is due to a lack of available teachers and also because the religion teachers are of the opinion that students should be introduced to elective programming only gradually. The following courses are offered on a semester basis. Students may choose two of the three courses.

1. "Christian Values and Modern Song." The students listen to and discuss the lyrics of contemporary songs in the light of Christian teaching. Various activity projects — questionnaires, surveys, interviews — are undertaken.
2. "The Meaning of Christian Maturity." This course treats of the process of human growth and human relationships in the light of Christian teaching.
3. "The Christian Interpretation of Current Events." The

"textbooks" for the course are popular Catholic and secular magazines. Discussions, panels, debates and activity projects are conducted.

Junior-Senior Years

The juniors and seniors are considered as one learning group. Over the period of their last two years in high school — four semesters — they may elect their courses from the following list of 11 offerings.

1. "The Pauline Epistles." Most of the students electing this course are high achievers. The course deals with the Pauline epistles in their historic context. Significant passages are interpreted and discussed.
2. "Cinema and Christian Values." Students view and discuss various films in the light of Christian belief.
3. "Doing Sacred Art and Drama." The teacher encourages the students to creative artistry concerning a religious theme. Selections of meaningful plays are performed and analyzed.
4. "Sociology of Religion." The great world religions and other value systems are studied from the viewpoint of sociology.
5. "Project." This "course" stresses almost exclusively the behavioral dimension of Christian education. Students engage in volunteer services such as work at hospitals, tutoring, etc., on a regular basis. Attendance at formal religious classes during the semester is not required.
6. "Revelation in Current Events." This course is a more advanced treatment of the themes covered in the sophomore class on current events.
7. "Faith and the Adolescent." Students study the phenomenon of believing — in biblical, historical and psychological perspectives.
8. "Self-study Program." Attendance at formal classes

is not required. The students, under the guidance of a mentor from the religion faculty, research a problem or prepare an extended theme.

9. "Literature and Christian Experience." Significant religious themes in modern literature are analyzed and discussed.

10. "Teilhard de Chardin: Religion and Science." This course attempts to understand the supposed conflict between religion and science against the backdrop of the life and work of Teilhard de Chardin.

11. "Christian Family Living." This is a marriage preparation course; an extended pre-Cana conference.

Students in the junior-senior group take one of the above courses each semester. They indicate their first three choices in advance of each semester, and the faculty attempts to schedule them according to the choices they have made. Courses are chosen in April for the fall semester, and in October for the spring semester. This gives teachers sufficient time for the preparation of the course, the placement of students and scheduling. Occasionally a student will request permission to take more than one course in a given semester. The faculty permits or disallows the choice on the basis of the student's ability and record.

Perhaps the most difficult problem in arranging an elective program is the recruitment of teachers to prepare an elective course from "the ground up." There are still too many religion teachers who wish merely to follow a textbook page by page. Each elective course must be planned with an eye to the concrete situation of the school; some courses cannot be offered at some high schools because of the dearth of materials or the lack of adequate facilities. Teachers are asked to employ a variety of textbooks and resources in the courses they develop. During the course of the school year the members of the religion faculty meet on a regular basis to search for better elective courses and to assist one another by sharing ideas and insights.

Despite the hard work and difficulties involved in arranging an elective program, most teachers and students agree that this approach is perhaps the most effective development in recent years in high school religious education.

The High School CCD

It has become increasingly evident over the past several years that many parish high school CCD programs are not meeting the challenge of providing good religious education for teenagers. Many programs are not attractive enough to attract good attendance. Some pastors estimate that less than half of the high school students in their parishes participate in the CCD program.

There are probably many reasons why some high school CCD programs are not effective. One of the major reasons, I think, is that the high school CCD program is modeled too closely on programs operative in Catholic high schools. Yet the difference between the Catholic high school and the parish CCD program, as I indicated above, is indeed great. In the Catholic high school the students are present for class every day of the school week; in the CCD program the students are present only one hour or so a week. Furthermore, those who come to the CCD class on a weekday evening have already spent most of the day in a school setting and they are emotionally exhausted, to some degree, by academic routine. If the CCD class is conducted on Saturday or Sunday, the students sometimes resent the intrusion of "school" into the weekend leisure period.

It should be recognized that in the CCD situation a serious emphasis on the cognitive dimension of Christian education will be unavailing. It would be unrealistic to demand homework of the students or to attempt anything more than brief coverage of doctrinal or theological issues. If textbooks of any kind are used, it is suggested that a "workbook" type be employed. The CCD situation permits some emphasis in the cognitive domain, I hasten to add, but not the same kind of emphasis which is congenial to the Catholic high school. An elective program in the parish high school CCD program, for example, is not impossible but highly improbable as an effective approach.

When I recommend the "workbook" type of text I mean such books as the series published by Herder and Herder: books such as *Friendship, Decision: Church, Involvement and Sex: A Book for Teenagers*. The Holt, Rinehart and Winston series *Conscience and Concern* is good, as is the Paulist *Discovery* series. Added to these materials I would also recommend the leaflet discussion stimulators produced by Alba House (*Life Topics*) and Pflaum Company (*Openers*). These materials suggest activities and points for discussion and offer questionnaires to be completed by the students. These materials do not require the reading effort demanded by the traditional textbook.

Classes should be informal and should accent discussion. Ideally the teacher-student ratio will be 1:8; the teacher serves as a discussion leader more than anything else and attempts to structure learning situations and an atmosphere which facilitates communication. At other times the discussion or "rap session" may be based on a film or a filmstrip, an audio tape or on the presentation of ideas of a guest speaker. In one parish all of the high school students met for a film or filmstrip in the parish hall and then divided into small groups under the supervision of a teacher to discuss the message of the filmic presentation. After discussion in small groups the students met again in the large grouping for reports of what took place in the small groups.

In a small parish the pastor invited the fifteen high school students in his parish to the living room of the rectory. The students viewed a filmstrip and conducted an informal discussion. Soft drinks and potato chips were always on hand, thereby helping to insure informality. Informality is important because it breaks down tensions which can become barriers to communication and impediments to learning. This informality and "non-school" atmosphere was achieved in one large parish by arranging for students to meet weekly in the homes of young couples who had volunteered as CCD teachers. During the course of the year all of the high school students would assemble for the liturgy, on three or four occasions, and for a dance or party in the parish hall.

Discussion approaches are not the only approaches that can be utilized for small groups. At times it may be feasible to work on a project, e.g., constructing a large collage or making a banner for the Sunday liturgy, visiting the sick in hospitals or the aged in nursing homes, preparing food baskets for the poor. One high school group studied the plight of the aged and produced a musical program at a retirement home. They visited with the elderly people and distributed small gifts.

In selecting films, audio tapes or filmstrips for the CCD program it sometimes happens that teachers worry about following a logical sequence of themes. They wish to treat the sacraments, for example, in seven successive classes. They should not hesitate, I suggest, to treat various themes in a nonsequential fashion. It is perfectly permissible to study life experiences in terms of the sacrament of baptism one week and to analyze current social problems the next. There is no absolute need to follow a pre-designed logical sequence of themes; the students themselves, in their own minds, are quite capable of tying things together logically. "We have generally assumed that logical consistency and a schematized approach to religious education is beneficial to students. I am not altogether convinced that this assumption is valid. It appears that a schematized approach to religious education is more helpful to a teacher than to a learner." [2]

Finally, I must mention an approach or structure for the

2. Cf. my article "Linear vs Modular Programming" in **A New Direction in High School Religious Education**, Jeffrey J. Schrank, S.M. (ed.), Argus Communications, Chicago, 1968, p. 13.

high school CCD that has shown promise in some large cities. The organization of the CCD program passes out of the hands of pastors and parish workers into the hands of a diocesan bureau. The bureau, composed of priests, religious and laity trained in modern catechesis, organizes study and discussion sessions at local Catholic high schools on Sunday mornings. In effect the Catholic high school becomes a student parish for all Catholic students in the district. The atmosphere is still informal and emphasizes discussion. After the time allotted to "class" the students gather for the liturgy. Relevant liturgies are conducted, and the students assist in selecting bible readings and devising liturgical actions which are meaningful to them. The homily is directed toward the students and not to a more general congregation as it is in the parish church. This approach seems to involve teenagers more profoundly in learning experiences and in the liturgy, while at the same time it undercuts the alienation sometimes experienced by youth in the parish church on Sundays. In other words, the students breathe in the atmosphere of a religious youth culture and not the religious culture of the adult world that is characteristic of the ordinary parish church. There are many limitations in this approach, but it is an approach worth experimentation.

My suggestions for high school structures have been ever so brief, but perhaps they will give some idea of the general approaches that can be followed with good results both in the Catholic high school and the CCD program.

Summary

The situation of the Catholic high school affords the opportunity of a greater emphasis on the cognitive dimension of Christian education than does the CCD program. This is not to say that the CCD program is less important or constitutes a less effective means of fostering the faith-growth of students. Different approaches must be used for the CCD program; failure

of many CCD programs results from too close an imitation of
the kind of learning that takes place in the Catholic high school.
Students enrolled in the CCD program must feel at ease, and
every attempt should be made to create an informal context
in CCD programs.

10

ADULT EDUCATION: PROCEEDURES

It is the contention of many catechetical writers and theologians that the Christian education of adults is of utmost importance. This contention is based on many reasons. If formal Christian education contributes to the faith-growth of people, we cannot call an end to this education simply because someone is an adult and out of school. Adults as well as children must grow and must strengthen their faith-relationship to God. We have worked on the unwarranted assumption in the past — at least some have worked on this assumption — that once a person finishes religious education in elementary, secondary or collegiate schools he is somehow a complete and perfect man. We know, however, that each person must continue to grow, mature and develop — in religious knowledge and attitudes and behavior as well as in other spheres of life.

The scarcity of Christian education programs for adults became quite evident in the wake of Vatican II. Much of the anxiety and turmoil experienced by some adults in the face of developments in Church life, i.e., liturgy, catechetics, theology, etc., can be attributed to the fact that these developments were not adequately explained to them. And explanations were not forthcoming in many places because of a lack of an educational setting for adults. The means of communicating the rationale for changes in the Church were not available; many adults were confronted with what appeared to them to be major changes and they were able to evaluate these changes only from the standpoint of a catechism education they received in childhood.

In emphasizing the importance of adult Christian education today some observers have called for an end of parochial education and the Catholic high school. It is not necessary, I suggest, to begin the construction of adult religious education programs on the rubble heap of existing educational structures. If a Catholic school offers inferior education, it should be closed; if a Catholic school unreasonably drains economic resources from other programs, it should be closed. But generally we should attempt to construct adult programs without first destroying present programs for children and adolescents. It is all too facile a solution to begin tearing down structures before adequate plans for new structures are outlined. Thus I am not too enthusiastic about phasing out this parochial school or that Catholic high school in favor of some ill-defined and vaguely delineated "catechetical center."

Our efforts in behalf of new programs and revitalized traditional programs for adults, however, should be redoubled. We can no longer simply ignore adults or treat them as second-class learners in the Christian community. This effort in behalf of adult Christian education should be carried out, as one writer has advised, for large groups and for small groups. I would interpret "large groups" to mean, first of all, a national audience. We should have educational programs for the masses. In this era of the blossoming of the means of public communication there is no reason to dismiss the possibility of near-universal religious education. Four annual documentary-type television shows, programmed at prime time on a national network, could help teach more than all of the Sunday morning radio and television productions of the past ten years. One feature-length motion picture, professionally executed and presented to the commercial market, would go a long way to assist millions of people to shape their attitudes according to Christian values.

Quite frankly I do not expect the Church in the United

States to produce anything worthwhile for prime time TV in the near future. Nor do I anticipate anything like the formation of a professional film production company. Such ventures would require the general collaboration of most of the bishops in the United States and a collective hierarchical vision of the future, not to mention the outlay of financial resources.

Until the possibilities of crossing dramatic frontiers in adult Christian education are not so remote, practical people would do well to concentrate their energies on the development of catechetical programs for "small groups" in the present-day dioceses, parishes and schools.

The process of adult Christian education for small groups — for a given number of people in a particular region or community — can follow an almost indefinite variety of patterns and procedures. The program that works best is one that has been tailored specifically for the real needs of a particular area or group. In the following paragraphs I will indicate several approaches to adult Christian education that have "worked" in certain places. The catechists who review these approaches can make adaptations necessary for their individual context.

Parents and Children

Some of the more successful religious education programs for adults have involved the recruitment of parents as catechists of their children. When parents are informed that they are responsible for the Christian education of their children in the home, and when they are given some assistance from priests and catechists, these parents spend much time in study and preparation. The adage that a person never really learns until he teaches proves true for most parents who find themselves cast in the role of catechists. In one parish there is no program for the children in the first three grades, at least no weekly program. Every two weeks the parents of the children in the first three grades meet with a trained catechist and are given some pointers on the Christian education of children. The children come together three or four times a year with their parents for a simple liturgy and celebration or "party" in the parish hall. This procedure has produced satisfactory results for the people involved.

Fortunately many of the newer textbooks for children involve parents at various levels of the catechetical experience. Any textbook series for children that does not involve parents is to be questioned. Such a textbook series fails to note the relationship between parents and children in the educational process. More to the point of this present chapter, such a textbook series ignores the fact that adults can be "reached" educationally in the educational activities of their children. The Paulist "Come to the Father" program merits special attention of catechists who wish to involve parents in the Christian education of their children.

The Lecture Approach

The lecture approach to adult education is quite traditional. With some innovative adaptations, it can be useful today. Guest speakers, panels, town-meeting-type sessions, dialogues or debates: all of these variations I group under the heading of lecture approach.

Here are a few guidelines to insure attendance and participation: 1) Charge a modest registration fee. People generally believe that what they get for nothing is worth exactly that. 2) List the titles of the lectures or panels, etc., in a printed leaflet. A printed prospectus gives a certain "class" and importance to the series. The titles of the lectures should be catchy but not hokey. 3) Never extend a lecture series beyond five sessions. Most people are willing to commit themselves to attend a series of talks or presentations as long as this series is not interminable. 4) Stipulate in the prospectus that no one will be asked to read anything, to answer questions or to pass tests. Many adults are willing to come and listen and reflect but they do not wish to get trapped in "school." 5) The best time to begin a lecture series is ordinarily toward the end of September and at the beginning of spring. People are ready to do something educational after long hot summers and long cold winters. In some places people are inclined to participate in educational programs even during the winter season, after the holidays and especially when lent begins.

Post-eucharistic Sessions

The practice of conducting discussion sessions in the parish hall after weekday evening Masses has been established in some parishes. In a few of these parishes filmstrips are shown in place of the homily on weekday evenings. After the celebration of the Eucharist the people meet in the parish hall for coffee, cookies and a discussion of the filmstrip. In still other places a short film is used in place of the homily and this film is discussed during the post-eucharistic session.

Post-eucharistic discussion sessions are also being conducted in some dioceses where the celebration of "home" Masses is promoted. One pastor informed me that he visits various neighborhoods or areas of his parish on a regular basis, celebrates Mass in a home and then conducts a discussion session. In another place the priest turns time over to a trained catechist who presents a program on one of the themes of the scripture readings. This program is then discussed by the people. The living room atmosphere is highly conducive to the sharing of insights and ideas. Not a few Christians of the Protestant traditions take part in the discussions which revolve around home Masses.

Post-eucharistic discussion sessions require that scripture readings for the Mass be carefully selected if these readings are to be the basis for discussion. The readings should come to bear upon a topic of current interest to the discussants. There are times, I think, when a catechetical experience can be linked productively to a liturgical experience by a wise choice of scriptural readings.

Film Festival

Several Catholic high schools have been known to sponsor film festivals as a program of adult religious education. The religion teachers of these schools attempt to increase the outreach of the high school to the parents of the students and to other interested adults in the surrounding neighborhood. One high school religion department provided a film festival as a "lenten series" a few years ago. Feature length motion pictures were shown on the Sunday evenings of lent. The religion faculty assisted as discussion leaders for the dialogues that took place after the showing of the films.

The "film festival" approach may have some possibilities for adult religious education in parishes. In the parish a team of publicists-organizers should be recruited from among the laity. They should help schedule films which will bring the viewers into contact with reality. These films need not be ostensibly religious. Nor is it necessary that they be feature length. The "Insight" films of Paulist Productions are not feature length but they are powerful dramatic statements that stimulate thought and discussion. Any film that explores human relationships and interactions in an artistic fashion can be utilized in a religious film festival. Or again, some of the films that were originally shown as television documentaries can bring people into contact with reality and can be employed to assist people in responding to situations in a precisely Christian manner.

At all costs the organizers of the film festival should avoid escapist cinema or those films that merely show a surface religiosity. Films such as "Going My Way," "The Bells of St. Mary's," "The Robe" or "The Ten Commandments" may have a religious veneer but they hardly qualify as significant religious cinematic statements.

The publicists should conduct telephone campaigns to inform members of the parish of the film festival. All too often announcements from the pulpit or in the parish bulletin are missed. Perhaps it may be necessary to supply local shops with posters advertising the film festival. This latter suggestion is of special significance when a group of local churches is presenting a film festival in ecumenical concert. Perhaps the organizers of the festival would do well to seek help from the parish youth groups in arranging a nursery to take care of the children of those parents who participate in the festival.

Those who help lead discussion of the films should view the films beforehand and discuss them with each other. Sometimes it is necessary to reproduce (ditto or mimeograph) discussion questions in order to get the discussion sessions moving.

Television Sessions

Occasionally television will produce an interesting and provocative documentary that can be exploited for the purpose of adult Christian education. Several years ago the documentary "Harvest of Shame" served as a springboard for discussion of the papal social encyclicals in one parish. The parish priest met with a small group of people who came together monthly as a discussion group. This meeting took place in one of the homes in the parish. The people viewed the documentary and discussed its statement in the light of Catholic social teaching.

The television networks supply a list of documentary presentations to schools; the list is mailed well in advance of the date of presentation to enable teachers to prepare classes around the documentary. It would be helpful if a team of resource persons be selected in the parish to check out the dates of important documentary programs and to inform discussion groups of these dates.

Mobile Units

In one diocese, after Vatican II, a team of speakers was organized to go from parish to parish explaining the various major documents of the Council. Each week a speaker would appear at a different parish meeting to offer his observations on an assigned theme. Discussions and questions would follow the address.

The diocesan or district religious education bureau usually organizes the programs and assigns speakers to the parishes. Some central coordinating effort must be forthcoming if mobile or traveling units are to function properly.

It is by no means necessary to restrict traveling units to addresses or formal lectures about a particular theme. Sometimes an individual or group of individuals may wish to present a film or filmstrip program. A group of high school students once created a sound-light program employing audio tapes, films and filmstrips; simultaneously, they projected colored light in the room and made use of strobe lights. The effect was what some people call "psychedelic." The program met with the applause of even very conservative groups of adults because it assisted them in gaining insights into the youth mentality and fostered discussion of a religious theme.

Discussion Groups

A more traditional approach to adult religious education is the discussion group. The groups meet at different homes in the parish. In some places national Catholic magazines or newspapers are used as a basis for discussion; in other places the familiar discussion club booklet, with questions interspersed in the text or after each chapter, is used. It is not necessary to employ a book which offers questions for discussion, but questions are sometimes helpful for people who are not adept at picking out the highlights of reading selections.

Parish Organizations

It was noted several times in previous chapters that people learn by doing and that behavior of certain types reinforces and supports the cognitive and emotional zones of religious education. A final word must be said, therefore, about the educational possibilities of parish organizations, or other organizations that are associated directly with religion.

Any organization that provides enriching experiences for its members can be said to be "educational." Thus, for example, the St. Vincent de Paul Society is an educational organization when its members learn or express sympathy with the poor. In the very act of helping others a charitable organization fosters the faith-growth of those who are involved in its program. The possibilities for education or for faith-growth are present whenever members of an organization are given the opportunity to be of service to others, to experience firsthand the problems of others or to witness a situation that elicits a Christian response. Unfortunately many religious organizations are more interested in mere fund-raising than in service projects which involve members directly in a situation demanding a Christian response. It is all very well to raise money for the poor by conducting a raffle; it would be better if the poor were served more directly by the members of a charitable organization. It would also be more beneficial to the process of adult religious education.

Summary

A growing number of Christian educators have recently underscored the importance of adult Christian education. Programs should be developed for large and small groups. While there is little hope at this time to finance national film programs or to obtain prime time television audiences, we can develop several programs for smaller groups. These include programs for parents which prepare them as home educators, lecture approaches, post-eucharistic discussion sessions, film festivals and so forth. Parish organizations now in operation can be educative agencies if members of these organizations become more personally involved in service projects.

11

DOCTRINE
IN CHRISTIAN EDUCATION

In some quarters today the warning of the author of the second letter of Peter is much in vogue: "... there shall be false teachers among you who will introduce destructive heresies ..." (2 P 2:1). In the aftermath of anything as historically dramatic as a General Council of the Church it is to be expected that those who possess a passion for the familiar will see false teachers lurking in ambush for the pilgrim Church. They will accuse religion teachers of watering down Church doctrine or dismissing doctrine altogether. "We must teach sound doctrine" has become the rallying cry of many contemporary Catholics who attack religion teachers who employ new approaches and techniques in the teaching of religion.

Honest solicitude for sound doctrine has also stirred the apprehensions of those responsible for the religious education of the young. I can sympathize with pastors and parents who have been overwhelmed by a deluge of new catechetical materials and puzzled by a multiplicity of new catechetical approaches. The educational patterns of today are simply not the same as the educational patterns of thirty or forty years ago. It is understandable that many people are alarmed about these changes.

In this chapter I wish to ask (and to answer) three questions: 1) What is doctrine? 2) What is the place of doctrine in Christian education? 3) Is it possible to discover truth oustide of specifically Roman Catholic or even Christian sources? Because of the complex nature of the first question, it will be necessary to devote more space to its answer.

What is Doctrine?

It is impossible to detail a comprehensive explanation of the meaning of "doctrine" in part of one chapter in a book. Such an endeavor deserves an entire volume. I wish only to suggest ten points about the notion of "doctrine" which may serve as fundamental concepts for further reflection about the meaning of "doctrine." The reader who wishes to study the notion of "doctrine" more profoundly should refer to the books mentioned in the notes for this chapter.

1. *The word "doctrine" is highly ambiguous.* Doctrine can be understood in many different senses. Quite simply, doctrine means "that which is taught." This is the generic meaning of the term. Under the heading of doctrine we can include everything from the proclamation of the resurrection of Jesus from the dead to the hortatory addresses which encourage people to participate more fully in eucharistic celebrations.

2. *Essential doctrines must be distinguished from private revelations.* One of the central teachings of the apostolic Church — "Jesus is Lord" — is of a different order than the quasi-official teachings in papal allocutions regarding the apparitions of Our Lady at Fatima. There is a substantial difference between the letters of St. Paul and the letter of Fatima. I mean here that we must not attach more value to private revelations than we do to essential doctrines. How we value essential doctrines *vis-a-vis* private revelations will be reflected in our religion classes.

3. *There is a gradation of importance among essential doctrines.* All essential doctrines are, by definition, essential to orthodox belief, but some essential doctrines are "hinge" doctrines. The doctrine that Jesus is Lord and Judge of history en-

joys a logical primacy over the teaching that the Church has received the power of remitting sins committed after baptism. All sacramental teachings hinge on the faith-affirmation that Jesus is Lord. It might also be mentioned here that there is a gray zone between essential and non-essential doctrines. Some doctrines are so remotely related to "hinge" doctrines that there is question among theologians whether these doctrines are essential or peripheral to orthodox Christian belief.

4. *Among essential doctrines there is a distinction between primary and secondary doctrines.* Some doctrines have undergone much reflection on the part of the Church over the centuries. These are called primary doctrines because they are theologically developed doctrines. Secondary doctrines are those which have not as yet been subjected to an in-depth investigation and interpretation by the Church.[1]

5. *Doctrines must be distinguished from the standpoint of the immediate source of the doctrine.* Traditional theology divided doctrinal statements into various categories: divine doctrines or ecclesiastical doctrines. Theological conclusions or conclusions based on reasoning about defined doctrines may be *close* to being necessary to belief, pertaining to faith, commonly accepted by theologians, probable opinions, pious opinions, or tolerated opinions. It must be noted that it is extremely difficult to categorize some theological conclusions despite the apparent ease with which this is done in theological handbooks.

6. *Some doctrines are mutable or changeable both in essential meaning and in the verbal formulation of the meaning.* Take, for example, the official, though non-dogmatic, teaching of Pope Boniface VIII in the papal bull *Unam Sanctam* (November, 1302). "We declare, state, define and pronounce that it is al-

1. For further clarification see Alis Winklhoffer's essay "Are Dogmas Subject to Historical Laws?" in **The Crisis of Change**, Chicago, 1969.

together necessary to salvation for every human creature to be subject to the Roman Pontiff." An explanation of the historic context of this pronouncement indicates that the subjection referred to by Boniface was to be interpreted as temporal as well as spiritual. This teaching or doctrine has obviously changed.[2]

7. *Some doctrines are immutable in essential meaning but mutable in terms of the verbal formulation of that meaning.* The real presence of Christ in the Eucharist, for example, was officially explained in words other than "transubstantiation" before the time of Innocent III and the Fourth Lateran Council (1215). While the essential meaning of the Eucharist pertains directly to the real presence of Christ, the formulation explaining *how* Christ is present obviously changed in the past. In other words, there is no hard and fast relationship between the reality of Christ's presence in the Eucharist and the words or formulations employed to explain theologically how Christ is really present.

8. *Doctrine is not revelation.* A doctrine is the propositional formulation or literary expression of a revelatory experience in the life of the Church. Revelatory events are first experienced; this experience of revelation is then put into ideas and framed in an official or formal statement.

It has been only in relatively recent times in the history of theology that the distinction between revelation and doctrinal statements has been clearly stated. In the past many people thought that revelation consisted of a collection of doctrinal statements. A good understanding of this distinction between doctrine and revelation will help settle many questions about the place of doctrine in Christian education. And perhaps one of the best volumes on this particular subject is Gabriel Moran's *Theology of Revelation.*[3]

2. The historical background of this question is constructed in Robert McNally's **Reform of the Church**, New York, 1963.

3. Moran's **Theology of Revelation** and its companion volume **Cate-**

9. *Doctrinal statements are time-conditioned.* The language in which a doctrinal statement is framed is, as Bruce Vawter puts it, "... subject to the attrition of time." [4] In traditional theology there always was the distinction made between the kernel of doctrine and the time-conditioned language in which this kernel was presented. Because doctrinal language changes, we must agree with Monika Hellwig when she writes: "In a formulation of doctrine there are usually many *possible* ways of expressing the truth; there has never really been only one correct way of doing it." [5]

10. *While the decisive revelatory events of the past cannot be repeated, revelation is ongoing: doctrine develops.* The Holy Spirit is with the Church as an active teacher of truth; the Holy Spirit assists the Church in the formulation of the Church's experience of revelation. Revelational experiences are ongoing, and the formulations of the Church's entire experience of revelation undergoes constant development.

We can see from the above ten points that it is not always easy to determine the soundness of doctrine presented in texts or taught by catechists. If we gain nothing else from this brief review of the meaning of "doctrine," we should realize that the notion of "doctrine" is extremely complex and not at all as easily defined as some people think.

What is the Place of Doctrine in Christian Education?

It may startle some people to learn that a good religion teacher does not teach doctrine; he teaches people. This holds

---

chesis of Revelation were published in 1966 by Herder and Herder. See also Theology of Revelation by Rene Latourelle, Staten Island, 1966.

4. Quoted in Bruce Vawter's excellent introduction to Herbert Haag's Is Original Sin in Scripture?, New York, 1969, p. 12.

5. Monika Hellwig, What Are the Theologians Saying?, Dayton, 1970, p. 9.

true in any other area of education. A good history teacher does not teach history; he teaches people about the reality of history. The distinction here may seem insignificant, but it is truly crucial. The difference between a good teacher and a drudge is largely determined by the manner in which the teacher approaches the educational situation, either from the standpoint of the people he will encounter or the abstractions he will cover. The teacher who teaches *people* will be able more easily to enter into a relationship of dialogue and friendship with the students; the teacher who teaches *religion*, or any other subject, will merely dole out informational data to students.

Christian education does not — directly, immediately and primarily — concern the increase of cognitional ability on the part of the students or the accumulation of abstract theological propositions. Christian education is fundamentally concerned about the faith-relationship of the students toward God, a relationship which develops ideally as the person develops and matures. Doctrinal statements which express the Church's experience of revelation find a place in the cognitive dimension of religious education as instruments or symbols which mediate to the students the Church's normative interpretation of revelation; doctrinal statements also serve as principles for the structuring of learning situations.

Doctrine is not learned for itself and in itself; doctrine is studied only insofar as it contributes to the vitality of the faith-relationship of the students toward God. This is not to say, I hasten to add, that doctrine is unimportant; it is supremely important. But it must be remembered that catechetics or religious education is distinct from theology; catechetics is not merely a form of diluted theology adapted for children, adolescents or the laity in general.

Essential doctrine is always at least *implicitly* involved in Christian education because essential doctrine serves as a guide or underlying rationale for the catechist in structuring learning situations which come to bear upon the emotional and attitudinal life of the students.

The extent to which doctrinal statements are studied *explicitly* depends 1) on the specific nature of the religion course and 2) on the age level of those under religious instruction.

Doctrinal statements may be studied explicitly, for example, in a Catholic high school religion class which focuses on the historical roots of modern ecclesiastical questions. On the other hand, doctrinal statements may not at all come into play explicitly in an elective religion course entitled, say, "Doing Sacred Art." It seems to me that the context of the weekly CCD session with high school students would prohibit any serious attempt to gain adequate understanding of all doctrinal statements. Most high school CCD classes are informal, as they ordinarily should be, and do not provide the day-to-day continuity which is necessary for the type of theological inquiry that promotes the development of the students' faith-relationship with God. A student may be able to memorize propositions, but the learning of doctrine is concerned with reflection and understanding and not simply memorization.

The age level of those under instruction also determines the extent to which doctrinal statements are explicitly treated. Quite obviously the catechist will avoid the study of complex doctrinal statements in dealing with small children. We must be cognizant of the clinical data of child psychologists. I cite two authorities: "In the stage of concrete operations, a child uses logic and reasoning in an elementary way, but he applies them *only* in the manipulation of concrete objects, not to verbal propositions." [6] " A great deal of religious thinking is propositional and therefore can only be dealt with at a formal operational level of thought, to be intellectually satisfying. If 13 or 14

6. Paul H. Mussen, **The Psychological Development of the Child,** Englewood Cliffs, N.J., 1965, p. 55.

is the mental age at which this level in religious thinking is generally achieved, a great deal of time and effort may be wasted by the instruction in ideas which are beyond the comprehension of the child." [7]

There is nothing more confusing to the child than a barrage of theological propositions which are beyond his ability of understanding. The so-called catechism approach to the religious education of children, for example, can be educationally counterproductive. Early catechetical experiences which induce confusion and boredom in the child may well cripple him emotionally in regard to the future learning of religious concepts and values. Furthermore, the catechism contains, as Karl Rahner points out, ". . . an undifferentiated mixture of dogmas, Catholic truths, truths that are theologically certain, and other material, all as seen by men rooted in their own times." [8]

I have mentioned in a previous chapter that many religious educators insist the catechetical programs for children which are now operative are much too cognitive. Generally the religious education of children is viewed in terms of education of the head, while the religious education of the heart is neglected. Perhaps this tendency to identify Christian education with the contents of the catechism is due to a mistaken notion of the catechism itself. Historically the catechism was never intended to be a textbook for children; it was originally intended to be a pulpit guide for preachers. "In concept, the catechism is a doctrinal handbook prescribed by bishops as a guide to their clergy in providing a pulpit catechesis." [9]

To sum up: Doctrine enters into Christian education, but sometimes only implicitly and minimally. The extent to which doctrine enters into Christian education explicitly is deter-

7. Ronald Goldman, **Religious Thinking from Childhood to Adolescence**, New York, 1968, p. 67.

8. Karl Rahner, **Theological Dictionary**, New York, 1968, p. 68.

9. Gerard Sloyan, **Shaping the Christian Message**, New York, 1963, p. 11.

mined by the nature of the religion course and/or the age level of the learners.

Where Can Truth Be Found?

The question of the sources of truth is usually brought forward by Roman Catholics. It is in this context that I shall attempt to answer the question.

Does truth exist outside of Roman Catholic sources? Can we hope to gain any insights into reality or aids for the Christian interpretation of reality from sources other than the pope, the bishops or Catholic theologians? Is the Holy Spirit operative only within the institution of the Roman Catholic Church? I feel most Catholics agree with Yves Congar when he writes: "If theology is always a question of reflecting upon faith, the type of theology wanted today is not so much the working out of this or that dogma of tradition, as the search for Christian understanding of the concrete experience of events and our encounter with other people. God reveals himself to us and calls us to him through men who are our brothers, and through the situations we meet in the world." [10] What Congar says of today's theology can be said also of today's Christian education.

There is much good to be found in the insights of non-Catholic philosophers, poets and artists and in the wisdom of many Protestant theologians.

Further, I suggest that the proclivity of contemporary theologians and catechists for examining the ideas of others (even non-Christians) is "traditional" Roman Catholicism in the best sense of the word. It was St. Thomas Aquinas, after all, who devised a Christian worldview for the people of his time by appropriating many of the fundamental insights of the pagan Aristotle.

Neither the catechist nor the whole Roman Catholic Church

10. Yves Congar, **Post-Ecumenical Christianity,** New York, 1970, p. 13.

can live on a mountaintop untouched by and impervious to the flux of life below. There is no such privileged pinnacle. The Church is a leaven which permeates the whole of life; the Church must rub elbows with the reality of life. St. Thomas did not fear to appropriate to Christ the insights of Aristotle, nor did St. Augustine hesitate to appropriate to Christ some of the central notions of the pagan philosopher Plato. Modern theology and catechetics must remain rooted in this tradition.

The catechist must take into consideration, then, the ideas which derive from non-Catholic or non-Christian sources. He will show either how these ideas contradict the gospel or how they can be appropriated to a Christian worldview that falls within the spectrum of Catholic orthodoxy. Nothing that is truly human or humanizing can be alien to authentic belief; nothing that is truly human or humanizing can be pushed out of the province of Christian education.

Summary

Three questions are asked in this chapter: What is doctrine? What is the place of doctrine in Christian education? Can truth be found outside of Roman Catholic or Christian sources? In answer to the first question we find that the notion of doctrine is very complicated. Several crucial distinctions must be made before we understand the meaning of doctrine. Doctrine is always present, at least implicitly, in the process of Christian education. Doctrine is treated explicitly to the degree that the nature of the course demands such explicit treatment and in accordance to the capacity of the students for abstract thinking. The tendency to assimilate truth and ideas from human culture is of long-standing Catholic tradition, since God is the author of truth wherever it is found.

12

AUDIOVISUALS
IN CHRISTIAN EDUCATION

The modern technological revolution is in some ways comparable to the industrial revolution of a century ago. Life-styles have been altered, older cultural patterns have been shattered or severely shaken, new products abound and novel approaches to problems have been uncovered. Nowhere is this more evident than in the area of education and, by extension, in the area of religious education. This is especially true in regard to the new "hardware" of religious education that is available today.

By "hardware" I mean the devices and instruments which promote better teaching and more enriched learning. These devices and instruments are usually referred to as audiovisual aids. The more sophisticated and complicated of these aids are now in the experimental stage; some of the so-called "teaching machines" presently in limited use represent the fruits of an advanced technology. But the cost of these machines prohibits mass purchasing. Economics has not as yet caught up with technology.

In some experimental schools, or in controlled educational programs operated by commercial enterprises, computers talk back to students, typewriters correct young typists who make mistakes in spelling, and teachers and students retrieve video cartridges which are inserted into individual television consoles much in the same way that books are selected in the traditional library. The influence of our technological culture on the methods and strategies of education has only begun to be felt.

I wish in this chapter to take note of some of the more ordinary audiovisual aids which can be used in the process of Christian education. Some of these aids will be more suitable for Catholic schools than for CCD programs; some aids will be more likely to be used for adults or high school students than for young children. The religion teacher must discern the utility of any particular audiovisual aid in the light of his specific catechetical circumstances.

Films

Although the motion picture is the child of an earlier stage of our technological culture, the use of films in religious education — to the extent they are being used today — signifies a departure from older patterns of religious education. During my twelve years of elementary and secondary education I can recall viewing a film in the school context on only two occasions. Today's students may view films on twelve occasions in the course of a semester, either in a Catholic school or in the CCD program. The educational impact of filmic approaches cannot be overestimated. A good film can phrase probing questions, provoke reflection, touch the viewers emotionally or call forth certain styles of behavior.

In religious education, films can be scheduled in two ways. A film may be integrated into the total plan for learning created by the teacher and students; or a film may be used nonsequentially, that is, with little or no relation to the learning experiences which precede or follow the showing of the film. In Catholic schools it is probably better to attempt to integrate a filmic presentation into the overall study plan. Since day-to-day continuity of learning does not obtain in the CCD program, it is futile to attempt to build strict continuity into lesson plans. A logical sequence or ordering of films according to an overall lesson plan is not necessary. In a weekly high school CCD program, for instance, the teacher may show a film concerning the generation gap one week and follow this up with a film on the problem of poverty the next week.

Following the showing of a film the students may wish to analyze and discuss its content in the light of their Christian interpretation of reality. The teacher should be prepared to offer guidance during the discussion session. Many books have been written concerning the use of films in religious education. The teacher should become acquainted with some of these books.[1]

For small children films should be used to provide a stimulus for affective development; that is, films should primarily entertain and elicit joyful or pleasurable feelings. Or to frame this advice in a different way, do not try to use films to support too much cognitive or intellectual development. We must constantly remind ourselves that children are not small-scale adults.

In most circumstances it will be impossible for schools or CCD programs to begin film libraries; the cost of motion pictures is quite high and the building of a film library requires a sizable financial outlay. It is advised, therefore, that the teacher rent films from the various places which specialize in film rentals to educational institutions. (A selected list of these places can be found in the appendix of this book.)

Filmstrips

In recent years the filmstrip has become a popular audiovisual approach to Christian education. While the filmstrip lacks the visual appeal of films or "moving" pictures, it does provide stimulating imagery at a cost substantially less than the cost

1. There are many books which deal with the use of films in religious education. I would recommend especially the chapter "Movies: The People's Bible" in Alfred McBride's **The Human Dimension of Catechetics** (Milwaukee: 1968). This chapter will serve as an excellent introduction to the way in which films can be exploited for use in Christian education.

of films. Filmstrips are sometimes produced without an audio component, i.e., a phonograph record or audio tape. In place of the sound portion of the filmstrip program, a reading script is supplied. The more popular and more effective of the filmstrip programs include an audio component synchronized with the visual part of the program. I may suggest that most of the filmstrips produced without an audio component are somewhat dated. It may cost a little more for a filmstrip-record program, but the expense is well worth it.

Because of the relatively low cost of filmstrips, it is possible for individual churches and schools to build filmstrip libraries. Over a period of four or five years, with skillful budgeting of financial resources, a good filmstrip library can be begun. It will be necessary, of course, to continue to add filmstrips to the library in subsequent years to maintain the availability of quality and current materials.

As with the selection of films, filmstrips should be selected which are appropriate to the capacities of the audiences. Children enjoy filmstrips that present a story. The Roa's filmstrip *Kree Finds the Way* or the Cathedral Films' series of filmstrips entitled *Parables of Nature* exemplify what I mean by "story" filmstrips. More advanced filmstrips which center attention on a particular theme can be shown to high school and adult groups to provoke discussion.

In many parts of the country, both in Catholic high schools and in CCD programs for adolescents, creative teachers assist students in making filmstrips which dramatize the "content" of what is being studied. Indeed, in some places the students even produce motion pictures, but such an enterprise is costly and technically difficult. All that is needed for a filmstrip is a script, a camera with color film, a cassette recorder and a projector. In many ways the involvement of students in the production of a filmstrip program can be greatly enriching for them.

Audio Tapes

Audio tapes have been a part of religious education for several years. Lectures, recorded by various experts on spools of magnetic tape, have been heard in classrooms and by adult discussion groups. Many religion teachers, unable to continue their own education in any other way, have depended on the audio tape to bring them the voices of theologians, educational theorists, psychologists, sociologists and other specialists. Over the past few years the audio tape has become more popular due to the invention of the cassette. The cassette or cartridge tape is not as unwieldly as the spool-type magnetic tape. Cassettes are much easier to store for future retrieval; cassettes can even be used by teachers to further their education while they are driving. Not a few people listen to recorded lectures in their automobiles. One CCD teacher told me that she listened to recorded theological, liturgical and scriptural talks while she worked in the kitchen during the day.

The teacher must exercise a good deal of caution when playing audio tapes for students or for discussion groups. Very often recorded lectures are transcribed at workshops which explore religious concepts in a detailed fashion. The lectures, therefore, are usually quite lengthy. While it is not too difficult to follow a speaker's train of thought when he is present — gestures and the speaker's facial expressions add an element of appeal to long talks — it is somewhat boring at times to listen to a taped transcript for any length of time. Tapes should never run over ten minutes when played back for groups of students. The chief function of audio tapes for groups is that they initiate discussion and the exchange of ideas of the members of the groups.

Audio tapes, especially the cassettes, are excellent for improving the means of independent study in schools. Some high schools have an audio tape section in their libraries. Students who are enrolled in independent study courses may retire to the library to listen to tapes in order to prepare a research paper or to prime themselves for a major oral quiz.

Records

An abundance of good phonograph recordings are available for catechetical use. Many of these records can be of assistance to the teacher who wishes to teach songs or hymns. It is far simpler for children to learn a song by first listening to a recording of the song than by trying to follow musical symbols on a printed page. For thousands of years people learned to sing their folk songs not by being able to read notes but by hearing the song over and over again. Singing is a very important part of the religious educational process for children, and the phonograph recordings of songs are invaluable aids for the teachers of children.

Then, too, music helps "set" an environment or atmosphere. Business learned long ago that a musical atmosphere helped increase the productivity of workers and assisted in relaxing prospective buyers in department stores. Education, and specifically religious education, should ask whether a musical background in some cases might not heighten potential for learning in students.

High school students sometimes enjoy listening to and then discussing the lyrics of folk songs. Not long ago I used a recording to call attention to the matter of Christian and human concern for the social injustices that are prevalent around the world today. After the students listened to a modern folk-song they discussed the reality of injustice in today's world in the light of the gospels and Pope Paul's encyclical *The Development of Peoples*. The recorded song was only part of a package that included salient documentation and prepared discussion questions.[2]

2. I am referring to the record-documentation package produced by Alba House Communications entitled **Dialogues for Self-fulfillment.**

At least one publisher of religion textbooks has developed a text which focuses on the meaning of modern popular songs.[3] High school students, and sometimes adults, generally find this approach appealing.

Overhead Projector

Using an overhead projector a teacher is enabled to illustrate an informative talk, project a visual stimulus to initiate discussion or even administer an examination. The overhead projector employs a heavy transparency resembling celluloid in the projection of an image. Designs, writing, maps and the like are imprinted on the transparency. The reflection of light projects the image on the transparency to a screen or white surface.

Some of the companies which produce overhead projector machinery also publish transparencies. While these mass produced transparencies are of good to excellent quality in many areas of education, the transparencies published for religious education are generally poor to very poor. It is better for the teacher to develop his own transparencies; "blank" transparencies and marking pencils can be purchased.

The overhead projector, together with the techniques involved in making suitable transparencies, sometimes poses problems for new teachers. Beginning teachers should be taught how to use the overhead projector by an experienced teacher. When new equipment is purchased, the purchaser for the school or CCD program should ask the manufacturing company to provide a representative to explain the mechanism of this audiovisual aid.

Opaque Projector

The opaque projector resembles the overhead projector, usually, in appearance, but the opaque projector is used for imaging

3. **Discovery in Song** is published by Paulist Press.

on a screen objects that are not transparent. Charts, three dimensional objects, entire pages of books: all of these can be focused on a screen for viewing by a group. The beginning teacher should have an introduction to the opaque projector that is more than merely casual. Nothing is more frustrating to a neophyte teacher than an unexplained piece of audiovisual equipment.

Some religion teachers produce exciting and interesting educational programs utilizing the overhead and opaque projectors. Other teachers hardly ever use these projectors. Whether or not the overhead and/or opaque projectors are compatible with a teacher's individual style is something that each teacher must learn from experimentation.

Television

The use of television in education holds many promises. Closed circuit television can supply many interesting opportunities for educational programming. Even more promising is the use of video tapes. Video tape works on the same principle as the audio tape. With a video tape recorder a teacher is able to transcribe, for example, an important night time television documentary for replay at any time. Students are given the opportunity of producing their own television shows which may range from "talk" shows to dramatic presentations. Video tapes may be stored for later use or even exchanged from one school to another.

The television camera and video taping offer almost unlimited possibilities for religious education in the 70's. Inhibiting factors in regard to television are 1) the absence or the shortage of creative religion teachers who will find ways of employing television in catechetics and 2) the present high cost of television equipment. Neither of these inhibiting factors presents us with insoluble problems, but undoubtedly the general use of effective educational television may yet be a decade away.

Banners — Bulletin Boards

Banners and bulletin boards, together with posters proclaiming insightful messages, can be helpful in the religion class. Sometimes an artistically designed and executed banner can encourage much reflection on the part of both teacher and students.

I will suggest two rules for the use of banners, bulletin boards and posters: 1) Do not allow these visual aids to grow stale. Change them every few days in a school situation and every week in a CCD situation. The impact of a banner, bulletin board or poster is greatly limited to the first time one of these displays is seen; 2) Do not purchase ready-made banners or posters. Students should be encouraged to develop their own classroom displays. This means that displays for the classroom will function both as visual aids and as activity projects.

Duplicated Materials

A year ago I taught a course to high school students entitled "Modern Adolescents and Belief." We examined the concept of faith, the religious psychology of adolescence and the relationship of the modern adolescent to the institutional Church. Since there was no satisfactory textbook available, I duplicated notes and outlines for the students each day. After the course was completed, several of the students told me that they liked the idea of having a collection of notes for references, and that the daily duplicated materials were helpful for them. The notes and outlines were distributed with the understanding that the students would not be responsible for the mere memorization of them. Indeed, the students were not coerced to avail themselves of the materials when they were distributed.

I mention this because many students today, despite their aversion for formal textbooks, still like to have some kind of printed word for the purpose of anchoring their thought processes. The question I wish to propose here concerns the type of duplicated materials that should be made available; that is, whether to use a spirit duplicating process or a mimeograph in preparing materials for distribution to students.

To prepare a master copy for the spirit duplicator, a person types (or writes) on the master with enough pressure to contact the underlying carbon sheet. A stencil is prepared for the mimeograph process. The spirit duplicator is much easier to use, but even the best master copy for the spirit duplicator can reproduce only 60 or 70 copies. In most educational situations this number of copies is sufficient. The mimeograph stencil is good for hundreds of copies. Also, the mimeograph stencil reproduces much clearer copies. Ordinarily I use the spirit duplicator because of the relative ease with which copies can be reproduced by this process. All teachers should become familiar with both duplicating processes.

Textbooks

Unfortunately we are accustomed to thinking of textbooks as containers of the "content" of religion classes; we do not ordinarily think of them as visual aids. Many teachers in the past, and many who are still teaching, have become enslaved to textual materials. Their idea of teaching is to read out of a text or to comment on the text, chapter and verse. We should recognize, however, that the textbook is one visual aid among many.

In an earlier chapter I noted that a good teacher is a creative teacher. A teacher of religion must never become tied down to one textbook. It is far better to employ an entire battery of textual materials for student research and reading at the high school level than to refer to only one book. In the early years of formal Christian education there is really no need for any textbook, although a basic text may be used. What is more important than the textbook to the teacher of children is the teacher's manual. Most teacher's manuals contain many excellent ideas for activities and projects for children. It is very important that teachers do not settle for one visual aid — the textbook — when so many different audio and visual aids are available.

Summary

In the foregoing paragraphs we have treated several of the more important and more popular audiovisual aids to learning. We have seen that learning, and teaching, can be enriched by a multiple use of available aids. We live in a culture in which communication takes place through technological means as well as by word of mouth. These technological instruments by which the word of mouth is amplified and the possibilities for communication are enhanced should become a part of the formal process of Christian education.

13

BUREAUS
FOR CHRISTIAN EDUCATION

In this chapter I wish to envision the ideal district or diocesan bureau for Christian education, a bureau that would contribute to the positive development of Christian education within
a given area. It takes more than the envisioning of ideals, it is
agreed, to precipitate desired changes in administrative structures. I realize, too, that not all religion teachers are directly
concerned with Christian education at the level of policy. But
many religion teachers are in positions to influence policy at
least indirectly by voicing their ideas to those who hold administrative offices in the Church. Changes in social and administrative structures are usually accomplished, I suggest, not
by those in the higher echelons of administration but by groups
of articulate people commonly referred to as the "rank and file."
If religion teachers merely wait for improved services from
a Christian education bureau, they will usually wait in vain.
This is not to say, of course, that all existing bureaus for Christian education are ineffective, but many are ineffective and we
should not hesitate to make such an observation.

Ideally a diocesan or district Christian education office
should define itself in terms of service. This office should be
a service apparatus of the diocese in matters pertaining to
Christian education and pastoral-educational care. The Christian education bureau should function: 1) to provide opportunities of continuing education for clergy, religious and lay

catechists, and to furnish the means by which teacher competency and qualifications may be judged; 2) to supply some of the educational hardware and make this hardware — films, filmstrips, audio tapes, etc. — available to teachers; 3) to help create organizational structures and educational programs for individual parishes and schools.

Continuing Education

The pace of change in religious education today is rapid. Newer and more effective approaches are being developed daily; newer and more effective tools of Christian education are being invented. This means that the religion teacher is challenged to keep abreast of what is happening. An office of Christian education could render service to many pastors and religion teachers by scheduling workshops and seminars in the diocese or at the district level within a diocese. Various speakers and experts in religious education, theology or communications should be invited to share their ideas with the religion teachers.

Some publishers of religion texts and materials are willing to send representatives to conduct workshops for prospective purchasers. The office of Christian education should arrange the details of these workshops, take care of the publicity and generally sponsor the meetings.

The staff of the bureau should feel responsible for providing ongoing programs of teacher assistance. These programs which help prepare beginning teachers and help keep veteran teachers informed can be sponsored by the bureau in conjunction with local church-related colleges or Catholic high schools.

In addition to the sponsorship of teacher training programs, the Christian education bureau should serve as a kind of accrediting agency for religion teachers. Certain guidelines for teacher competency, developed by the religion teachers themselves for the bureau, should be promulgated. Basic minimum qualifications should be expected of religion teachers. Religion teachers should be certified only after they have attended a workshop, completed a correspondence course or made some other significant effort to achieve proficiency. The willing spirit of the volunteer teacher is to be praised, but sometimes enthusiasm for teaching is the only qualification demanded of a teacher, with the ensuing result of poor teaching and hardly any learning.

Minimum qualifications — stated by a committee of active religion teachers — should be met not only by volunteer lay teachers but also by clergy and religious. It may not be very politic to say this, but honesty must be served: not a few pastors and religious are quite unfit, either by temperament or training, to function as religion teachers. The bane of many religion classes has been the clergyman who inflicts utter boredom upon students by reading to them the notes he took of seminary lectures, or by rehashing something out of a theological manual. Simply because a man is a priest or minister, simply because a man or a woman is a religious, we should not suppose that he or she is a competent religion teacher.

Continuing education for religious teachers can also be fostered through a monthly newsletter published by the bureau of Christian education. This newsletter could contain brief reviews of books, notices of special events such as workshops in the general vicinity, comments of religion teachers on new methods and techniques, and digests of important articles that have appeared in journals and magazines. Some newsletters I have seen offer very little help to the religion teacher simply because the newsletter is conceived of merely as an instrument for the publication of mandates and decrees. The bureau of Christian education should always keep a clear image of the newsletter as a "help" for religion teachers.

Educational Hardware

The Christian education office should procure and make available some of the physical resources of Christian education, resources which assist in teacher preparation and which can be used in creative learning situations for students.

The bureau should maintain a lending library of relevant books. There are many important theological and catechetical books on the market; there are many audio tapes that are instructive for teachers. But it is almost impossible for the individual religion teacher to purchase most of these enrichment resources. After gathering together a representative collection of books and audio tapes, the bureau should publish a listing of materials in the library for distribution to the teachers. Subsequent additions to the library can be published in the monthly newsletter. In dioceses of large area it may be possible to establish substation libraries or to make materials available through the mail.

Just as it is difficult for any individual to buy all of the necessary books and magazines published today, so also is it next to impossible — particularly in small rural parishes — for a parish to obtain all of the necessary films, filmstrips, records and other audiovisual materials that constitute the hardware of Christian education. The Christian education office would do well to build a library of those materials which can be used by the teacher for the benefit of the students. Parochial schools, CCD programs, Catholic high schools and adult study groups could all draw on the materials.

The central audiovisual library must be well stocked, and duplicate copies of popular items should be obtained. In one diocese the central audiovisual library purchased several copies of seasonal materials — filmstrips on Advent liturgy, Christmas and Easter films, etc. It is self-defeating to begin a library with a paucity of items. Patrons of the library lose interest after they have been told several times that the audiovisual materials they wish to borrow are out on loan.

Structures and Programs

Most importantly the Christian education bureau must serve as a center for consultation. Pastors should be able to call upon the staff of the bureau to assist in devising the organizational structures and educational programs for parishes and/or schools. The inner-city school is different from the suburban or rural school; the CCD program is not the same as that of a parochial school; an adult education program in one parish may be unsuitable in an adjacent parish.

Each parish should develop its own organizational structures for Christian education from the ground up and should seek the assistance of the members of the diocesan bureau for Christian education. Should there be a committee of laity to work with the religion teachers? Who should be committee members? Who will take charge of transportation for the children? How can the CCD program be publicized? What kind of budget will be necessary for an effective Christian education program in the parish school? These and similar questions can be answered only after the concrete situation has been analyzed and studied.

Other questions are of an educational nature. What kind of program best meets the needs of this parish? What textbooks are available for the CCD program or parish school? Are these textbooks suitable? Should this particular high school experiment with an elective program in religious studies? What discussion themes can be selected that would be most advantageous for the people of this parish? Program development is always important, and all too often program development is a hit-and-miss affair. The result is educational stagnation. The religion teachers and people involved in programs of Christian education should have an opportunity to consult with professional specialists in religious education who have access to the most recent information about materials and trends.

The consultants from the diocesan bureau are not to be envisaged as designers of programs who work in isolation from the religion teachers and people who live in a particular situation. On the contrary, most of the work of creating organizational structures and educational programs must be done by those directly involved in a given situation. Acting as consultants the staff members give advice, familiarize religion teachers and people with recent developments, disseminate information on materials, provide personal evaluations and present models of programs that have proven effective in other places.

In his book *The Making of a Counter Culture* Theodore Roszak decries "elitist managerialism"and laments the tendency in our culture to defer in every decision to those "who know better." The staff members of the Christian education bureau must never become elite managers, and religion teachers and people must participate fully in the decision-making processes by which organizational structures and educational programs are initiated.

The Bureau Staff

The number of staff members in the Christian education bureau depends on the size of the diocese or district. Most diocesan bureaus today present us with a paradoxical situation. Having worked in a Chancery, and having observed others closely, I know that too many people are usually employed at unimportant tasks and busywork, while too few people are engaged in important matters. In some diocesan bureaus the bureaucrats spend most of their time finding ways of doing work that does not have to be done; in most Christian education bureaus there are not enough staff members to deal with the work load. At any rate, each individual place must solve its own problem as to the number of staff members necessary for an efficient operation.

The staff members should be professional in the sense that they have received special preparation in religious education, in communications and/or that they have shown some degree of competence in the areas of religious education. A *sine qua non* for members of the staff is a temperament that permits them to work effectively with people. Any number of excellent plans and programs have met with failure because those who proposed the plans and programs did not know how to get along with people.

There are two ways, I believe, to insure good relationships between staff members of the Christian education bureau and religion teachers: 1) a representation of the religion teachers themselves on the staff of the bureau and 2) the establishment of channels of communication between the staff and the religion teachers.

In these days of what is called the "democratization" of the Church there seems to be no good reason why the religion teachers — at an annual meeting or by mail vote — should not be permitted to elect representatives to serve with the staff of the bureau of Christian education. The religion teacher or teachers who were elected to a staff position could learn something of the administration aspect of education and could serve as liaison between the "rank and file" and the administrators of the bureau.

Staff members themselves, whether an elected religion teacher serves on the staff or not, should be vigorously concerned about the input of communication from the religion teachers. If the staff is dedicated to serve the religion teachers, it stands to reason that it must keep open the channels of communication through which the religion teachers may express their needs and problems. Again, many an excellent program has failed because of the inability of staff members to address themselves to the specific needs of pastors and religion teachers. This inability may derive from the fact that staff members of the bureau were not listening to the religion teachers and pastors, or from the fact that channels of communication were not established to permit listening.

Finances

Perhaps the most difficult question relating to bureaus of Christian education is the question of finances. How does a diocese finance a bureau, pay the salaries of staff members and purchase materials for both a teacher resource library and an audiovisual library? I will not pretend to know the answers to these questions. I would propose the general observation, however, that financial and moral support is not lacking to those bureaus of Christian education that perform real service for the parishes and religion teachers of a diocese. If the bureau is a mere "official" office which does not really serve the needs of Christian education, it deserves neither the financial support of the diocese nor the moral support of the religion teachers. If the bureau earnestly attempts to provide service, moral support will gather. And in the wake of moral support, usually, financial support will follow.

A final observation about the financing of the bureau of Christian education: new priorities for financing administrative bureaus must be established. The financial problems of educational bureaus are tied in with the much larger problem of diocesan priorities in funding various operations. It seems to me that no diocese can afford not to fund a bureau of Christian education. The Church, after all, does have a teaching mission. And this mission can be accomplished effectively when diocesan funds are spent to create the kind of bureau of Christian education I have envisioned in this chapter.

Summary

Religion teachers themselves can help reorganize administrative offices of Christian education by sharing their ideas and insights with officials. Religion teachers should be keenly interested in the bureau of Christian education which serves the catechetical needs of the diocese. Ideally the Christian education bureau defines itself in terms of service; it sponsors programs for the continuing education of pastors and religion teachers, it provides educational hardware such as audiovisual aids, and it serves as a center for consultation. The problem of financing the operations of the bureau of Christian education is formidable, but not so formidable that it cannot be overcome by a bureau which provides real service, and by a reordering of funding priorities in each diocese.

14

LITURGY AND CHRISTIAN EDUCATION

From time immemorial man has celebrated the great events and awesome moments of his life with symbolic gestures and ritual. In early tribal societies men were fascinated by the element of the "extraordinary" in their lives and celebrated extraordinary times and events with ritual activity. Apparently most men, modern men as well as primitive tribesmen, are moved to do something special to mark a birth, a coming of age, a marriage or a death; somehow men feel as if they should behave in a dramatic way to take note of the advent of spring, the gathering of a harvest or the beginning of the winter months. Seasonal celebrations, usually bearing some reference to religious belief, have been an almost constant factor in the history of man's social development and organization.

In devising rituals to celebrate an extraordinary event men have relied on their symbol-making abilities. Symbols are used to express the inexpressible and to utter what cannot be put into mere words. I remember being quite impressed as a small child when I witnessed a ceremonial of brotherhood in a western movie. The cowboys and the Indians, embattled for most of the film, finally settled their differences and agreed to live together in peace. On the screen the Indian chief and cowboy hero cut their wrists with a knife and then placed their wrists together, indicating an intermingling of blood and symbolizing the beginning of friendship. The passing of the peace pipe among American Indians to symbolize an agreement is another symbol employed in rituals of friendship. In many cultures a covenant or pact was celebrated by the sharing of a meal; the meal continued to be shared year after year commemorating the original covenant. This commemorative meal not only marked an anniversary but effectively suffused the participants with feelings of peace, harmony and fellowship.

The symbolic gestures of ritual were common among primitive men, especially in the area of religious concern and belief. The people would re-enact symbolically and ritually a myth which described the deeds of a god. Primitive men lifted themselves out of the ordinary course of human events and somehow exorcised the terrors of life by recourse to sacred ritual. The symbolic gestures of ritual worship became a special way of re-experiencing the great deeds of a god or hero; ritual became a means of expressing attitudes toward the god or hero.

Early in its development the ritual would be rather freewheeling and spontaneous; the symbolic gestures of the ritual were fixed only loosely to the core theme of the myth which was being ritualized. Ritual, in its beginnings, was flexible and no rigid rules for the ritual were prescribed; ritual expressed the most profound needs and feelings of the people who participated rather actively in the ritual.

As the social organization of the tribal society became more and more developed, and as ritual became institutionalized, precise rules for ritual behavior were mandated. The symbolic gestures of the ritual became less spontaneous. Ritual behavior was guided by the religious leaders and no longer *expressed* the attitudes of the people; ritual activity was employed by the religious leaders to *elicit* attitudes from the people.[1]

The symbolic gestures employed in religious ritual, even after the ritual had become institutionalized, were laden with

1. For an interesting and concise sociological analysis of the meaning of ritual see Thomas F. O'Dea's **The Sociology of Religion**, Englewood Cliffs, New Jersey, 1966, pp. 40ff.

the power to transform and instruct. A symbolic gesture brings together in a single act a multitude of ideas and feelings. A handshake between friends, for example, "says" many things that cannot be put into words. Only when a symbol or symbolic gesture becomes a matter of mere convention does the symbol lose its power to effect transformation and to communicate meaningfully. Of itself the control of ritual behavior by religious leaders — the institutionalization of ritual — is not necessarily all bad. Rules for ritual behavior become a necessity in large groups to prevent the ritual from falling into a state of chaos. Only when the *meaning* of the symbolic gestures is overshadowed or betrayed by the rules for the gestures does ritual begin to suffer degeneration.

Christian Liturgy

Perhaps Christians can find much help for keeping their liturgies vital and meaningful through a sociological analysis of ritual. Christians dramatize certain events in life ritually, much as did their pre-Christian ancestors; Christians celebrate the salvational deeds of Christ much in the same way that primitive men celebrated the great deeds of their gods and heroes. There is a difference, I affirm, between the ritual of pre-Christian men and the Christian liturgies. Whereas pre-Christian men recounted in ritual the deeds of gods who never were, Christians testify in their liturgies to the deeds of the living God who really entered the process of history in Jesus Christ. The events celebrated by Christians truly occurred in human history and not merely in the creative imaginations of poets.

What is interesting about the sociology of ritual, at least in the context of this chapter, is the knowledge that ritual begins as a more or less spontaneous expression of belief and religious feeling on the part of the people and then tends to become — with the onset of institutionalization — a less flexible and less spontaneous type of behavior which is intended to elicit belief and religious feeling. This matter is very important for Christians today — especially Roman Catholics — who are experiencing changes and transitions in liturgical style and form. In the light of recent liturgical changes we could almost postulate a sociological theory which states that when ritual becomes too highly stylized and controlled, the people will resort to liturgies which are more spontaneous and truly expressive of their feelings. The so-called "underground" Masses did not come into being in a sociological vacuum.

At the last supper Jesus employed the already existing ritual of the Passover Meal as the occasion for instituting a new ritual which focused on his death and resurrection. This ritual or liturgy is variously called the Mass, the Lord's Supper or the Eucharist. For convenience I shall refer to the liturgy simply as the Mass.

At its very initiation the Mass was not formless nor was it totally devoid of structure. In early Christianity, however, the celebration of Mass was not highly stylized; there was room for spontaneity on the part of the people, and the rules governing the celebration of the Mass were not rigidly enforced. A small community of Christians would celebrate Mass in such a way that they could respond personally to their experience of the risen Christ, and in this response they would express their attitudes of faith, hope and love.

Only later in the history of the Church, after the Church had grown in numbers and began to develop some kind of social organization, was the ritual of the Mass institutionalized. The Mass became a means of eliciting from the people, especially after the mass conversions of the barbarians, attitudes of faith, hope and love.

This analysis of the Mass in sociological terms, however brief it may be, gives us some understanding of the problems confronting Christians today concerning the liturgy; specifically it helps religion teachers to examine the liturgy in its relationship to Christian education. Should the Mass principally express the religious attitudes of the people, or should it elicit or "call forth" religious attitudes? Should the Mass, or any Christian liturgy, involve the people more intensely and permit greater spontaneity, or should it be more highly stylized? How these questions are answered will come to bear upon strategies for Christian education.

Liturgy: Expression and Elicitation

We must beware of either-or questions and we must be cautious about having alternatives forced upon us. The question "Is the purpose of the liturgy to express or to elicit religious attitudes?" is a false question because it presumes liturgical behavior cannot at the same time express and elicit faith, hope and love. The liturgies of the sacraments and the liturgy of the Mass both express and elicit religious attitudes, but not uniformly for all people and in all circumstances.

In small informal groups the liturgy of the Mass may very well present possibilities for expression of religious attitudes and may allow for much spontaneity. In larger and more formal groups the liturgy can provide some kind of "call" to attitudes of conversion. In other words, there are different styles of liturgy and there are different levels of participation in the liturgy. These different and varied styles and levels of participation are conducive to different and varied outcomes.

We need not tear down church buildings in favor of small-group liturgies for everyone; we need not discourage small-group liturgies and herd all people into church buildings. The desideratum is, I think, that people — adults, adolescents and children — be provided with the opportunities of participating in the liturgy at as many levels of participation as is feasible. The religion teacher will, therefore, attempt to structure occasions for liturgical experiences which range from the small, spontaneous and informal liturgies celebrated in the home to the large, highly stylized and formal liturgies celebrated in the great cathedrals. I can sympathize with renewalists in Christian education and in the liturgy who are opposed to any "spectator" theory of participation in the Mass. And I certainly prefer personally to celebrate Mass informally and under conditions which permit spontaneity. But I have no desire to impose my liturgical tastes on everyone, least of all my students. As a religion teacher and not as an indoctrinator, I feel obliged to structure a variety of liturgical experiences for my students.

The enrichment of liturgical experience for the learners need not concern only those liturgies which have official approbation of the leaders of the Church. Liturgical celebrations of all kinds can be devised for celebration in the home, school and church building. These celebrations, which are more properly called "para-liturgical," also possess power to transform and to touch the hearts of the participants. Semi-official "devotions" have always played a part in the Christian education of people in the history of the Church.

Liturgy in the Home

Learning experiences in the home constitute the foundation for all subsequent learning experiences. This implies that parents provide learning experiences in the home which contribute to the Christian and human development of their children. Again, we return to a previously stated axiom: a child cannot be educated in isolation from his parents or those who are parent surrogates in the home. I propose here that the early (pre-school) Christian education of children should take place largely through home liturgical experiences, and that these experiences be continued in the home while the child is advancing toward adulthood.

The home paschal meal, the advent wreath, the pentecostal wheel, the celebration of name days, family prayer, the home easter candle and the ritual surrounding it, the blessing of the Christmas crib and tree: all of these activities can contribute to the Christian education of both children and parents.[2] It

2. Lawrence E. Moser, S.J., has written a very helpful book regarding

matters little whether the child understands the significance of these liturgies in an abstract way. The language of ritual or liturgy bypasses the ordinary rational avenues and is addressed to the "heart" — to the affective side of the human personality.

Liturgy in School

Liturgical experiences in the context of the learner's peer group are likewise valuable. This does not mean that children in the parochial school or CCD program should be regimented into the church building for liturgies they are not prepared to celebrate. Too often in the past, particularly where a parochial school was concerned, the pastor would line up the children and take them as a captive audience into the church building for Mass. Such a practice of lockstep piety only leaves the children with unfavorable impressions. It would be informative if someone would trace the relationship between some modern adolescents' aversion for Mass and their experiences of childhood regarding forced attendance at Mass. Those who attempted to build mechanical "good habits" in children perhaps only succeeded in alienating them, in later years, from liturgy.

The liturgy in the parochial school or the CCD program — aside from Sunday worship — should be informal, relaxed and suitable to the mental capacities of the children. As the child moves from the lower and middle grade levels into the upper grade levels and high school, he should be invited to involve himself ever more in the planning of the liturgy: in the selection of the theme of the liturgy, the choice of readings and songs and the composition of the prayers.

The liturgical activity should take place ordinarily in the school building or the place of CCD instruction, and generally in small groups. This last suggestion is made to insure informality, relaxation and spontaneity. Many children and adoles-

---

liturgy in the home. It is entitled **Home Celebrations**, New York, 1970, (Paulist Press).

cents identify the church building with more formal and stylized liturgies. Liturgical celebrations in the church building — on Sunday, for example — will provide exposure of more formal and stylized liturgies.

Liturgy in the Church Building

The celebration of the liturgy by the entire parish community — given the manner in which parishes are organized today — poses a dilemma. If the liturgy is oriented toward the adults, the children and adolescents may feel left out. The scriptural readings and homily will be too advanced for children and at times irrelevant to the felt needs of the adolescents. On the other hand, if different liturgies are created specifically for children, adolescents and adults, there is a danger that children and adolescents may never experience initiation into the total parish community; they may begin to feel even more alienated from the total parish community precisely because they do not celebrate the liturgy with the adults. Finally, if the liturgy is addressed partially to children, partially to adolescents and partially to adults, the liturgy itself will suffer.[3]

Liturgy As Model Christian Education

The Christian liturgy is a model or exemplar of what Christian education should be like. That is to say, the philosophy of Christian education, I believe, must derive fundamentally from a study of Christian liturgy. Earlier I mentioned that the process of Christian education involves three distinct domains of the human personality: the cognitive, the affective and the be-

3. This a real dilemma and presently I see no solution given by the Third Instruction on the Liturgy. In section 2b we read: "The liturgy of the word prepares the assembly and leads them to the celebration of the Eucharist. Thus the two parts of the Mass form one act of worship and may not be celebrated separately, at different times or in different places."

havioral. Knowledge, feeling and activity ideally come into play in the process of Christian education. Nowhere is this convergence of knowledge, feeling and activity more obvious than in the liturgy. Scripture readings, songs, the homily, symbolic gesture and ritual movement: all of these are ingredients of an educative process which is concerned with cognitive, affective and behavioral results. The liturgical actions of Christians, then, must be viewed as the necessary cognate of Christian education. I conclude this book with a brief essay on liturgy not because liturgy is some kind of afterthought, but because Christian education can be understood only in reference to Christian liturgy.

Summary

Ritual plays an important part in man's life. Ritual is used to express religious attitudes and to elicit these attitudes. Formality is introduced into ritual when ritual becomes institutionalized. A study of the liturgy from the standpoint of sociology is helpful for understanding some of the liturgical questions being asked today.

In general there should be many different forms of Christian liturgy. The form of the liturgical celebration should take its origin out of the situation in which the liturgy is celebrated. Students should be enabled to participate in varied forms of Christian liturgy.

Christian liturgy represents a model for understanding the ideal process of Christian education. That is to say, Christian liturgy is addressed to the cognitive, affective and behavioral domains of the human personality.

APPENDICES

SELECTED READING LIST

The following list of books does not represent itself as an exhaustive bibliography for the religion teacher. For the sake of keeping the list as brief as possible, the titles of many books used in the preparation of the foregoing chapters do not appear here. Some of the books in this reading list are not directly concerned with Christian education but offer ideas and insights which may be helpful for the beginning religion teacher.

Audinet, Jacques
Forming the Faith of Adolescents, Herder and Herder, New York, 1968.
Babin, Pierre
Methods, Herder and Herder, New York and Palm Publishers, Montreal, 1967.
Options, Herder and Herder, New York and Palm Publishers, Montreal, 1967.
Adolescents in Search of a New Church, Herder and Herder, New York, 1969.
Audiovisuals, Pflaum, Dayton, Ohio, 1970.
Bergevin, Paul; Morris, Dwight, and Smith, Robert M.
Adult Education Procedures, Seabury, New York, 1963.
Bixler, Lawrence
How to Teach, Standard, Andover, Mass., 1964.
Brusselmans, Christiane
Religion for Little Children, A Parents' Guide, Our Sunday Visitor, Huntington, Indiana, 1970.
Carroll, James P.
Feed My Lambs, Pflaum, Dayton, Ohio, 1964.
Castagnola, Lawrence, S.J.
Confessions of a Catechist, Alba House, New York, 1970.
Coudreau, Francois, P.S.S.
Basic Catechetical Perspectives, Paulist, New York, 1969.

Cruchon, Georges
  The Transformation of Childhood, Pflaum, Dayton, Ohio, 1969.
Cully, Cris V.
  Children in the Church, Westminster, Philadelphia, Pa., 1960.
Curran, Charles E.
  A New Look at Christian Morality, Fides, Notre Dame, Indiana, 1970.
Curran, Dolores
  Do Not Fold, Staple or Mutilate, Ave Maria Press, Notre Dame, Indiana, 1970.
  What, Me Teach My Child Religion?, A Catholic Parent's Viewpoint, Mine Publications, Minneapolis, Minn., 55403, 1970.
Daglish, William A. (ed.)
  Media for Christian Formation, Pflaum, Dayton, Ohio, 1969.
  Media Two, Pflaum, Dayton, Ohio, 1970.
Doherty, Sister M. Michael, I.H.M.
  Dynamic Approaches to Teaching High School Religion, Alba House, New York and Palm Publishers, Montreal, 1968.
Goldman, Ronald
  Readiness for Religion, Seabury, New York, 1968.
  Religious Thinking from Childhood to Adolescence, Seabury, New York, 1968.
Havighurst, Robert J.
  The Education Mission of the Church, Westminster, Philadelphia, Pa., 1965.
Hellwig, Monika
  What Are the Theologians Saying?, Pflaum, Dayton, Ohio, 1970.
Howe, Reuel L.
  The Miracle of Dialogue, Seabury, New York, 1963.
Hubbard, Celia (ed.)
  Let's See: The Use and Misuse of Visual Arts in Religious Education, Paulist, New York, 1966.

Jeep, Elizabeth
Classroom Creativity, Herder and Herder, New York, 1970.
Larsen, Earnest, C.SS.R., and Galvin, Patricia, C.S.J.
Will Religion Make Sense to Your Child?, Liguorian, Liguori Missouri, 1970.
Lee, R. S.
Your Growing Child and Religion, Macmillan, New York, 1963.
Lee, James M., and Rooney, Patrick (eds.)
Toward a Future for Religious Education, Pflaum, Dayton, Ohio, 1970.
Lorentz, Deborah, S.S.S., and Schwab, Elwin
Ideas for Electives in High School Religion, Pflaum, Dayton, Ohio, 1970.
Mariella, Sister
What Have They Done to the Catechism?, Paulist, New York, 1970.
McBride, Alfred
Catechetics: A Theology of Proclamation, Bruce, Milwaukee, 1966.
The Human Dimension of Catechetics, Bruce, Milwaukee, 1969.
McBrien, Richard P.
Church: The Continuing Quest, Paulist, New York, 1970.
McIntyre, Marie (ed.)
Aids for Religion Teachers: Some Procedures and Techniques, Our Sunday Visitor, Huntington, Indiana, 1968.
Aids for Religious Teachers: Teaching Teens, Our Sunday Visitor, Huntington, Indiana, 1968.
Parents: Educators at Home, Ave Maria Press, Notre Dame, Indiana, 1969.
McKenzie, John L.
The Roman Catholic Church, Doubleday Image, New York, 1971.
McKenzie, Leon
Process Catechetics, Paulist, New York, 1970.

Montessori, Maria
    The Discovery of the Child, Fides, Notre Dame, Indiana,
    1957.
Moran, Gabriel, F.S.C.
    Catechesis of Revelation, Herder and Herder, New York,
    1966.
    Theology of Revelation, Herder and Herder, New York and
    Palm Publishers, Montreal, 1966.
Mueller, Alois (ed.)
    Catechetics for the Future, Herder and Herder, New York,
    1970.
Mussen, Paul H.
    The Psychological Development of the Child, Prentice-Hall,
    Englewood Cliffs, New Jersey, 1963.
Newland, Mary Reed
    Homemade Christians, Pflaum, Dayton, Ohio, 1964.
O'Neill, Robert, and Donovan, Michael
    Children, Church & God, Corpus, Washington, D.C., 1970.
Oraison, Marc
    Love or Constraint?, Paulist, New York, 1959.
    Morality for Our Time, Doubleday, Garden City, Long Is-
    land, New York, 1966.
Orem, R. C. (ed.)
    A Montessori Handbook, Putnam, New York, 1966.
Pitlyk, Jean, C.S.J.
    Media in High School Religion: A Journal, Pflaum, Dayton,
    Ohio, 1970.
Ranwez, Pierre
    The Dawn of the Christian Life, Paulist, New York, 1970.
Reichert, Richard
    Xpand: Experiencing Christianity, Ave Maria Press, Notre
    Dame, Indiana, 1970.
Russell, Letty M.
    Christian Education in Mission, Westminster, Philadelphia,
    Pa., 1967.

Ryan, Mary Perkins, and Neighbor, Russell J. (eds.)
There's More Than One Way to Teach Religion, Paulist, New York, 1970.
Schrank, Jeffrey J., S.M.
A New Direction in High School Religious Education, Argus, Chicago, Illinois, 1968.
Seeber, George E., S.J.
CCD Sundays, Ave Maria Press, Notre Dame, Indiana, 1967.
Scott, Vaile
Adult Education, Argus, Chicago, Illinois, 1968.
van Caster, Marcel, and le Du, Jean
Experiential Catechetics, Paulist, New York, 1970.
Vergote, Antoine
The Religious Man, Pflaum, Dayton, Ohio, 1969.
Wyman, Richard
Mediaware: Selection, Operation and Maintenance, Brown, Dubuque, Iowa, 1969.

PERIODICALS

The following periodicals can be of great assistance to all religion teachers. Again, I have tried to select only the most helpful of the many religious periodicals available.

The Living Light
Noll Plaza
Huntington, Indiana 46750

The Catechist
38 West Fifth Street
Dayton, Ohio 45402

Religion Teacher's Journal
P. O. Box 180
West Mystic, Connecticut 06388

The Parent-Educator
P. O. Box 180
West Mystic, Connecticut 06388

Religious Education
545 W. 111th Street
New York, New York 10025

Mass Media Ministries
2116 N. Charles Street
Baltimore, Maryland 21218

AUDIOVISUAL SOURCES

Abbey Press (Liturgical programs)
St. Meinrad, Indiana 47577

Alba House (Books, filmstrips, records, audio tapes)
2187 Victory Boulevard
Staten Island, New York 10314

Alba House Communications (Books, films, filmstrips, records and audio tapes)
Canfield, Ohio 44406

Argus Communications (Audio tapes)
3505 N. Ashland Avenue
Chicago, Illinois 60657

Association Films
25358 Cypress Avenue
Hayward, Calif. 94544

Avant Garde Records
250 W. 57th Street
New York, New York 10019

Brandon Films
221 W. 57th Street
New York, New York 10019

Carousel Films
1501 Broadway
New York, New York 10036

Catechetical Guild (Filmstrips)
262 E. 4th Street
St. Paul, Minn. 55101

Cathedral Films (Films, filmstrips)
2921 W. Alameda Avenue
Burbank, Calif. 91505

Contemporary Films
1714 Stockton Street
San Francisco, Calif. 94133

John P. Daleiden Co. (Filmstrips)
1530 N. Sedgwick Street
Chicago, Illinois 60610

Family Films and Filmstrips
5823 Santa Monica Boulevard
Hollywood, Calif. 90029

Family Theater (Films)
7201 Sunset Boulevard
Hollywood, Calif. 90020

Guidance Associates (Filmstrips)
23 Washington Avenue
Pleasantville, New York 10570

Insight Films (Films and audio tapes)
Paulist Productions
17575 Pacific Coast Highway
Pacific Palisades, Calif. 90272

Kairos Films
6412 Indian Hills Road
Minneapolis, Minn. 55435

Thomas S. Klise, Inc. (Filmstrips)
P. O. Box 3418
Peoria, Illinois 61414

Koinonia Records
617 Custer Street
Evanston, Illinois 60202

Life Filmstrips
Time-Life Building
Rockefeller Center
New York, New York 10020

Liturgical Press (Liturgical programs)
St. John's Abbey
Collegeville, Minn. 56321

Mass Media Ministries (Films)
2116 N. Charles Street
Baltimore, Maryland 21218

Geo. A. Pflaum, Publisher (Filmstrips, audio tapes)
38 West Fifth Street
Dayton, Ohio 45402

Roa's Films (Films, filmstrips)
1696 N. Astor Street
Milwaukee, Wisconsin 53202

St. Francis Productions (Films)
1229 S. Santee Street
Los Angeles, Calif. 90015

Sterling Educational Films
241 E. 34th Street
New York, New York 10016

(The companies listed above offer films on a rental basis. Filmstrips must be purchased. Audio tapes are usually purchased, but occasionally a company will provide rental tapes. At this writing only Paulist Productions offer audio tapes on a rental basis.)